# 31 DAYS
## of a
## *Servant's*
## HEART

*Desiree Smith White*

# 31 DAYS of a Servant's HEART

**Copyright @ 2024 Desiree Smith White**
**ISBN: 979-8-9904970-4-7**
**All rights reserved.**

Author owns complete rights to this book and may be contacted in regards to distribution. Printed in the United States of America.

**Library of Congress Cataloging-in-Publication Data**

The copyright laws of the United States of America protect this book. No part of this publication may be reproduced or stored in a retrieval system for commercial gain or profit.

No part of this publication may be stored electronically or otherwise transmitted in any form or by any means (electronic, photocopy, recording) without written permission of the author except as provided by USA copyright law.

**The Holy Bible:** New King James Version. Thomas Nelson. NB 1982 (NKJV)
**The Poems:** All poems created and owned by author: Desiree Smith White

**SHEROPUBLISHING.COM**

Editing: SynergyEd Consulting/ synergyedconsulting.com
Graphics: Greenlight Creations Graphics Designs
glightcreations.com/ glightcreations@gmail.com
Book Cover: SHERO Publishing

# 31 DAYS of a *Servant's* HEART

### Desiree Smith White

## Table of Contents

| | | |
|---|---|---|
| Dedication | | 7 |
| Acknowledgments | | 8 |
| Foreword | | 10 |
| Introduction | | 11 |

## 31 Day Devotional

| | | |
|---|---|---|
| Day 1 | God Issued an Amber Alert for Me | 12 |
| Day 2 | God's Witness Protection Program | 16 |
| Day 3 | Faith Begins Where Explanation Ends | 20 |
| Poem | To My Treadmill | 24 |
| Poem | Tyree Day Cento | 25 |
| Day 4 | I've Got Your Back | 26 |
| Day 5 | Sin Has Collateral Damage | 30 |
| Day 6 | You Don't Have to Understand to Trust | 34 |
| Poem | Hidden in Plain Sight | 39 |
| Day 7 | Building Your Life from the Inside Out ... | 40 |
| Poem | The Butterfly | 43 |
| Day 8 | That Same Jesus | 44 |
| Day 9 | Stuck Where You Stopped | 48 |
| Day 10 | Good Does Not Mean Saved | 52 |
| Poem | Zuihitsu Poetry | 56 |
| Poem | Retirement | 57 |
| Day 11 | All Means Everyone | 58 |
| Day 12 | You're Under Consideration | 62 |
| Day 13 | Mother, Where Art Thou? | 66 |
| Poem | And Baby Needs a Pair of Shoes | 70 |
| Poem | Haiku Sonnet | 71 |
| Day 14 | Is that Your Final Answer? | 72 |
| Day 15 | I'll Make Room for Jesus | 76 |
| Day 16 | The Holy Spirit Sensor | 80 |
| Day 17 | Make Room to Learn | 84 |

## Table of Contents
### (Continued-Page 2)

### 31 Day Devotional

| | | |
|---|---|---|
| Day 18 | God Always Has a Batter on Deck | 88 |
| Poem | Daybreak | 93 |
| Day 19 | Go and Sin No More | 94 |
| Poem | Fairview Neighborhood | 99 |
| Day 20 | Constructed with Success in Mind | 100 |
| Day 21 | Set Up for Victory | 104 |
| Poem | The Church and The Black Church Experience | 109 |
| Day 22 | It's Up to You | 110 |
| Poem | Ode to the Harmonic Refined Lady | 115 |
| Day 23 | You're Missing the Good Part | 116 |
| Poem | Expectations | 121 |
| Day 24 | Adversity is the Bridge to Growth | 122 |
| Poem | Her Child | 127 |
| Day 25 | Let the Spirit Lead | 128 |
| Day 26 | A Change Has Come Over Me | 132 |
| Day 27 | Lessons Learned from a Widow | 136 |
| Day 28 | Looking Good on the Way to Hell | 140 |
| Poem | Journey to Healing | 145 |
| Day 29 | The Need for Gap Protection | 146 |
| Day 30 | He Paid Full Price | 150 |
| Day 31 | The Goal is to Go Home | 154 |
| About | Author Desiree Smith White | 159 |

# 31 DAYS of a *Servant's* HEART

*Desiree Smith White*

# *Dedication*

To My Beautiful Children
Elden and Tatum

Thank you for extending to me the privilege of being your mother. You have given me joy, purpose and inspiration. It is my prayer that these devotions will enrich your lives, draw you closer to God and provide confirmation that I have been listening to the beats of your hearts.

I love you to life!

# Acknowledgments

With sincere appreciation *(I didn't do this by myself):*

- ❖ To God and His Son Jesus, for allowing me to be beautifully and wonderfully made in your image; for speaking to my heart and my head and for showing up on every page of this book.

- ❖ To my mother, Amelia Earhart Smith, for the countless hours you read to me as a child, showed up at school to make sure teachers knew you were an involved parent, instilled in me a spirit of excellence and taught me the ways of the Lord.

- ❖ To my late father, James Horatuies Smith, for making me believe I could do anything if I put God first, encouraging me to never give up, supplying the resources I needed and showing me how to wear my garment of praise.

- ❖ To my sister, Tara, for always having my back and believing in what God called me to do. You are a phenomenal sister, friend and confidante.

- ❖ To my late husband, Bishop Elden D. White, for helping me to recognize God's call to service upon my life and increase my faith. Nineteen years of marriage anchored me during times of trials and triumph.

- ❖ To my teachers and professors for expecting me to give the best I had to offer and for using their red ballpoint pens to correct my English papers to help me become a proficient and creative writer.

- ❖ To the Allen's Chapel Missionary Baptist Church for your role in providing a Christian foundation. Special gratitude to Pastor Emeritus James W. Brown, the late Cumillia Farrish Vanhook, Deborah Woods Fuller, and Elizabeth Farrish Woods for giving me confidence and helping me face my fears.

- ❖ To Rev. Dr. Larry E. Covington for welcoming me into the body of Christ at The Ebenezer Church and for supplying a platform for me to exercise my ministry gifts the way God packaged them for me. Your visionary leadership and teaching of sound biblical doctrine, along with the members of Ebenezer, have blessed me beyond measure.

- ❖ To the prayer warriors of *"It's in My Heart"* Mid-week Devotion for joining me on the conference line each Wednesday at 6:15 a.m. Your words of gratitude and support provided me strength to finish this assignment.

# Foreword

I am deeply honored and humbled by the request of Reverend Desiree Smith White - a friend, a fellow preacher of the gospel whom I have the greatest respect for and one whom I have had the pleasure of pastoring for these last five years - to write the foreword for this wonderful ministry gift in print titled, *"31 Days of a Servant's Heart"*.

Reverend White, within the contents of this must-read book, uses her professional scholarship as a writer. She draws upon her inspiration as a worshiper. She skillfully combines her unique journey as a woman, a wife and a mother, with her knowledge of the Word of God to present to the reader daily doses of practical and applicable devotional studies. Each daily devotion will motivate and stimulate one on their spiritual pilgrimage to know Christ in a more intimate way and to serve Him with a servant's heart.

I really love Rev. White's unique way of illustrating her subject matter using real-life scenarios from the pages of the news and from her life. Like Jesus' usage of the parables, Rev. White makes sure that the reader is able to identify with the subject matter. Through her use of stories, illustrations and terms that are familiar, she enhances the spiritual lessons that are being shared in each of her daily devotional readings. Treat this book as a bottle of spiritual vitamins that should be taken every day to aid in your spiritual health!

I pray this beautiful, practical and spiritual devotional book will be an important resource to each of us. To some, I pray that it will be a starting point of a daily quiet time with the Lord. To others, it will be a challenge to refocus and recalibrate that which is spiritual as a daily priority and as a companion to scripture. And for all of us who are readers of this work, may it serve as a support and a guide to aid us in our daily journey towards wholeness and holiness.

Enjoy and be enlightened!


Rev. Dr. Larry E. Covington
The Ebenezer Church, Burlington, NC 27217

# Introduction

To My Readers:

Welcome to *"31 Days of a Servant's Heart"* – a month-long devotional designed to help you strengthen your walk with God through an understandable and uplifting explanation of the gospel.

Alongside the Bible, this devotional will provide you daily insights applicable to everyday experiences, pensive moments and prayers that will allow you to deepen your relationship with God. Whether you are a seasoned saint, new to the faith or not a believer in God at all, if you read these devotions with an open mind and a willing heart, they will cause you to pause and think about life and a relationship with your Creator with a fresh perspective.

On this 31-day journey, it is my fervent prayer that these pages will reveal my desire to be obedient to the Word of God, lead others toward a relationship with God and provide a clear explanation of the gospel message leading you, as the reader, to develop a hunger and thirst for righteousness. May this book prompt you to look through the lens of faith and think about where you will spend eternity.

Enjoy every breath of today as you travel this pilgrimage of discovery.

Desiree Smith White

# DAY 1

# God Issued an Amber Alert for Me

**Scripture Reading:**    Luke 19: 1-10

*For the Son of Man has come to seek and to save that which was lost.*
                                                            Luke 19:10

**Daily Devotion:**

In 1996, nine-year-old Amber Hagerman was abducted from her grandmother's neighborhood in Texas while riding her bicycle. Four days later, she was found murdered, and her killer was never located. Yet, Amber Hagerman has become known worldwide. Her abduction inspired the AMBER alert, an acronym for America's Missing Broadcast Emergency Response alert. Active in all fifty states and in dozens of countries, this alert system distributes details about child abductions via digital highway signs, radio, television and wireless devices when a child is abducted and expected to be in immediate danger. To date, the program has saved over 1100 children.

In the summer of 1974, long before AMBER was ever an official child recovery system, an alert was issued for an eleven-year-old girl. She was not physically missing, but according to God's Word, she was not in a place of safety, having not accepted Jesus Christ as the Savior of the World. So, God, through his Son Jesus, instructed the Lord to get this little girl. He issued a Holy Spirit Amber alert. And while Jesus was in the neighborhood, God asked Him to get the girl's sister as well. God had work for them to do. God knew that people would say they were too young to be used by Him; however, just as anglers use minnows to catch bigger fish, God had plans to use these little vessels as bait for a larger catch. At times, these sisters would feel swallowed up, but just like Jonah, their survival was part of His plan. God knew there were others who were lost, and God needed them to find a place to call home. The two sisters had no idea why they were tapped for the kingdom cause, but they were willing.

Fast forward to the present day to meet me and my sister Tara, now adult women, who are still being used by God as bait – prayerfully in a spirit of humility letting our lights shine while leading others to Christ. If you are reading this book and you are saved, you are in the position of spiritual safety because a Holy Spirit AMBER alert was issued for you. You were lost and couldn't find your way home. You were in imminent danger with no hope of escaping on your own. You were working at the pleasure of the enemy because a failure to accept Jesus Christ as Savior puts you in the employment of the devil by default. If you don't choose God, the devil chooses you. But when the Holy Spirit AMBER alert was issued, Jesus came looking for you. And because you didn't resist, you are now on your way to your eternal home. It may not be today or tomorrow, but when God calls your name, there is a place waiting just for you – the place of the Glory of God. But for now, you are being used as spiritual bait – not to be eaten by larger fish – but to lure lost fish from the swampy pond of the enemy to a heavenly aquarium where the devourer cannot live. The place of 12 gates and 12 foundations – where the Garden of Eden has been restored; where nations are healed; death is conquered, and the Lord is present.

In the scripture, Jesus has an encounter with Zacchaeus. And when this tax collector learned that Jesus wanted to stay at his house, he repented of his wrongdoing, gave back what did not belong to him, and he was saved. Jesus issued an AMBER alert for Zacchaeus. This tax collector wanted to be found.

God, whom we serve, comes to seek and to save the lost.

# Daily Reflections

**Pensive Moment:**

Do you remember when you were lost, and an AMBER alert was issued for you?

**Prayer for Today:**

*Precious Father,*
*Thank you for your Holy Spirit alert system that came looking for me when I needed to be found.*

**Daily Thoughts/Goals:**

_____

_____

_____

_____

_____

_____

# DAY 2

# God's Witness Protection Plan

**Scripture Reading:** Luke 23: 39-43

*And Jesus said to him, "Assuredly, I say to you, today you will be with Me in Paradise.* Luke 23:43

**Daily Devotion:**

The Organized Crime and Control Act of 1970 authorized the Witness Protection Program, also known as the Witness Security Program. The purpose is to protect federal witnesses whose lives may be in danger as a result of their cooperation with the federal government. The program ensures their security, safety and health by giving the witness a new name, a change of location and a place of protection to allow them to testify without worry of harm.

In our scripture, we meet two thieves who are hanging alongside Jesus waiting to experience the painful death of crucifixion. However, one of the thieves is about to receive witness protection. He knows he is guilty but, unlike his cohort, he decides to be a witness for the Lord. He tells his friend that they are receiving just punishment for their deeds because they are responsible for what they did, but Jesus has done nothing wrong. This thief turns to Jesus and says, *"Lord, remember me when you come into your kingdom."* Jesus responds, *"Assuredly, I say to you, today you will be with Me in Paradise."*

From Jesus' response, we can glean that God extended His protection to this accused man – the witness who acknowledged Jesus and His innocence. Being with Jesus in Paradise was a promise to the thief that his sins were forgiven, and he would inherit eternal life.

Just like the federal government Witness Protection Program,
- God will **give you a new name**, which will lead to new beginnings, new hopes and new blessings. He changed Abram to Abraham; Sarai to Sarah; Jacob to Israel; Simon to Peter.
- God will **change your location** to accomplish His will. He sent Abraham to an unknown land. He sent Moses to Egypt. He sent Jonah to Nineveh. He sent Ruth to the homeland of Naomi.
- God will **provide protection**. He protected Noah and his family from the flood; the widow at Zarephath and her son from starvation; Shadrach, Meshach and Abednego from the fiery furnace; Joseph from the wrath of his brothers; Jonah from being digested by a fish.

As Christians, our lives are in danger as we declare ourselves witnesses for God and His Word. Under the New Covenant with Jesus, we are not guaranteed physical safety, but if we have God's spiritual protection, like the thief, we will be with Him in Paradise.

# Daily Reflections

**Pensive Moment:**

With Jesus hanging in between, would you be the thief on the left or the thief on the right?

**Prayer for Today:**

*Precious Father,*
*Provide unto me the courage to stand before the masses and declare with boldness, power and authority that I am YOUR witness.*

**Daily Thoughts/Goals:**

_____

_____

_____

_____

_____

_____

# DAY 3

# Faith Begins Where Explanation Ends

**Scripture Reading:** Proverbs 3: 1-35

*Trust in the Lord with all your heart and lean not on your own understanding.* Proverbs 3:5

**Daily Devotion:**

When I was a student in school, particularly in my elementary and middle school years, I was very inquisitive. I wasn't satisfied with knowing the time on the clock. I wanted to understand how the watch was made and the name of the manufacturer. My teachers applauded me for my work, but there were times when they suggested that I made things more difficult than they needed to be.

Math was always a challenge. In Algebra, I experienced difficulty understanding how A plus B could equal C. Why were we trying to add letters of the alphabet? In Geometry, word problems caused me even more anxiety. For example, if Little Leroy walked to school at three miles per hour, and the school was four miles away, how long did it take Little Leroy to walk to school? While my classmates were figuring out the answer to the problem, I was asking the teacher why Little Leroy was walking to school by himself in the first place, and why didn't he just ride the bus? At that time, I believed there was an explanation for everything, and if I studied enough, I could make whatever I questioned logical in my mind. That is, until I came into spiritual contact with the Omniscient, Omnipresent, Omnipotent Lord of Lords and King of Kings - Jesus Christ.

Christian apologetics is the science of defending your faith. All Christians should be able to provide a level of defense for why we believe what we believe. But I realized that as I read the Bible and attended Sunday School and Bible Study, there were aspects of God and His Son Jesus that I could not explain. The Bible states that God created the heavens and the earth. Easily, the question becomes, "Who created God?" But God falls into the category of something that is neither created nor caused. God simply exists. And if you are one of those persons who believes that God had to be made or created to exist, in all likelihood, you will not be able to believe in Him because you cannot explain how He got here. The Word of God tells us to lean not to thine own understanding, which affirms there will be situations that we will not be able to articulate and or explain poised on our human rationale and intellect. God is that category.

Many precepts of the Bible must be accepted through the lens of faith, which means that we trust in things that we cannot see and accept events and circumstances that we may not be able to explain with human logic.

We don't see oxygen in the air we breathe, but we need it to live. Without it, we die. We really don't care if we see it as long as we have it. We don't see air in a bag of potato chips, but when we open the bag, and it deflates with only a few chips inside, that's evidence that something else was in the bag. We didn't see it, but it was there. We call it air. Where God is concerned, many people have convinced themselves that they must see or be able to explain God to believe Him. But God is like the air in a bag of chips. He may not be seen with the naked eye, or explained, but the absence of Him creates a void.

After a few struggles, I understood the Algebra problem, and with Little Leroy, the only thing that mattered was he arrived at school. Where God is concerned, I don't have a complete comprehension of how He works. But I am thankful that He works. I still have questions that no one can answer, but my faith begins where explanation ends, and that is more than enough for me.

# Daily Reflections

**Pensive Moment:**

Are you willing to accept, with faith, the things you cannot explain?

**Prayer for Today:**

*Precious Father,*
*Thank you for Your Son, Jesus, who died for my sins. He loves me unconditionally, and I love Him whether I can explain Him or not.*

**Daily Thoughts/Goals:**

_____

_____

_____

_____

_____

_____

# To My Treadmill

when I look at you
sitting in the corner of my office gathering dust
I wonder how different
my life would be
had we continued our affair

early in the morning
before others would rise
we met

with my heart beating rapidly
and perspiration dripping
down my neck and in the small of my back
I enjoyed every part of you

you wanted only to make me
look and feel good
but I needed more

I had no rivals
then you did
and the more you beckoned me to come
he beckoned me more

he is my mattress
I choose to sleep

# Tyree Day Cento

I began to pray
in the house of my mother

My mama would say
boy you better make sure
no prayer I give you will end

What I pray for
Lives under an ash tree

Mama still.

# DAY 4

# I've Got Your Back

**Scripture Reading:**    Ecclesiastes 4:9-12

*Two are better than one because they have a good reward for their labor.*
                                                        Ecclesiastes 4:9

**Daily Devotion:**

For the first 11 years of my life, I lived in a community known as Fairview, located in Hillsborough, North Carolina. My parents rented a little green cinderblock house where my sister Tara and I shared a bedroom.

We slept in a double bed that seemed huge at the time. At night, my dad would tuck us into bed. He would insist that we sleep with our faces in opposite directions, so our backs were pressed against each other. He said sleeping back-to-back would help us stay warm and keep the cool draft of the room from coming between us.

I didn't understand, at the time, because the room was always comfortable to me. But my dad grew up with wood stoves and fireplaces and multiple children sharing one bed, huddling together to keep warm. With that knowledge, my sister and I did as he asked. There was comfort in knowing that Tara "had my back." That is, I could always count on her to be there for me no matter what I needed.

Eventually, we left the Fairview Community and the double bed in the little greenhouse for a bigger house with twin beds in a new neighborhood. Shortly thereafter, I had my own room. When my dad tucked us in individually, I could no longer feel Tara's back against mine. It was not the same, but I never felt alone. Knowingly or unknowingly, my dad's insistence that we sleep back-to-back as kids created a bond that continues to exist between me and my sister. We grew up to live our own lives in separate locations. Yet, somehow, I know she still "has my back."

That is precisely the way it is with God. After we declare our love for Him by repenting of our sins and accepting His gift of salvation, He has our backs. Nothing can separate us from Him at that point, for we are "sealed to the day of redemption." He loves us unconditionally and is always there when we need Him. And while life provides us with "temperature" changes in the form of trials and situations we endure, God protects us through the draft – life's harsh consequences. God keeps us joy-filled during the most challenging times.

The scripture reads, "Two are better than one because they have a good reward for their labor." It was not good for Adam to live alone, so God gave him Eve, a helpmeet. Despite their differences, Eve had Adam's back. Jesus had 12 apostles and sent them out to do the work of the kingdom in pairs. They had each other's backs. Moses had a brother named Aaron; Naomi had a daughter-in-law named Ruth; Paul had a friend named Timothy.

Each of us needs someone who will have our back – who will lift us up, help us out and provide encouragement when we need it.

# Daily Reflections

**Pensive Moment:**

In what ways are you providing support to the Kingdom of God and to those you love?

**Prayer for Today:**

*Precious Father,*
*Thank you for providing "back" support when I needed it most.*

**Daily Thoughts/Goals:**

_____

_____

_____

_____

_____

_____

_____

# DAY 5

# Sin Has Collateral Damage

**Scripture Reading:**  Genesis 3:1-19

*To the woman He said: 'I will greatly multiply your sorrow and your conception; in pain you shall bring forth children; your desire shall be for your husband, and he shall rule over you.' Then to Adam He said, 'Because you have heeded the voice of your wife and have eaten from the tree of which I commanded you, saying you shall not eat of it': cursed is the ground for your sake; in toil you shall eat of it all the days of your life.*
Genesis 3:16-17

**Daily Devotion:**

When injury, hurt or harm is inflicted upon innocent people, the result is collateral damage – pain or death to an unintended target. A good example of collateral damage occurs when countries are at war. There are always innocent bystanders who are harmed. Like war, sin harms. It hurts. It causes collateral damage.

Often, I hear the statement, you're hurting "no one but yourself." But that is utter nonsense. If you have ever loved anyone, you know sin hurts and can have unintended consequences for innocent people.

In the scripture, we are in the Garden of Eden with a man named Adam, who was the keeper of the Garden, and a woman named Eve, Adam's helpmeet. They have been given dominion over the Garden with the responsibility to tend and keep it. But there was one stipulation. God told them they could not eat the fruit of a certain tree. If they did, they would die. Adam and Eve did not follow the instructions. They collapsed under the pressure of their flesh and made the decision to eat the fruit that was forbidden.

God disciplined Adam and Eve for their disobedience. Yet, the discipline did not affect only Adam and Eve but their offspring. Death exists in the world today because Adam and Eve sinned. And it broke the heart of God, their Creator. Two people caused collateral damage for all of humankind.

Sin does not merely hurt the sinner. Sin has repercussions that extend beyond the one who commits the offense.

- ❖ The person who chose to drive drunk, resulting in an accident that led to a fatality, caused collateral damage.
- ❖ The teenager who had unprotected sex and is now a parent with no means of support caused collateral damage.
- ❖ The employee who embezzled money from the company and lost their job caused collateral damage.
- ❖ The illnesses and diseases that result in missed time from work, sometimes unpaid, caused collateral damage.
- ❖ The lies told that hurt another's reputation caused collateral damage.
- ❖ The crime committed that led to jail time and required someone else to pay the bail caused collateral damage.

Every time you sin, you hurt the heart of God and of those who love you. So, the next time you feel compelled to hurt "nobody but yourself," remember you are causing collateral damage.

# Daily Reflections

**Pensive Moment:**

*What sin in your life is causing collateral damage?*

**Prayer for Today:**

*Precious Father,*
*Help me to resist the temptation to sin, as I am not the only one affected.*

**Daily Thoughts/Goals:**

_____

_____

_____

_____

_____

_____

# DAY 6

# You Don't Have to Understand to Trust

**Scripture Reading:** Proverbs 3:1-12

*Trust in the Lord with all your heart and lean not to thine own understanding. In all your ways acknowledge Him, and He shall direct your paths.* Proverbs 3:5-6

**Daily Devotion:**

I remember the day like yesterday. It was a Monday just after 12:00 noon when my mobile phone rang. My sister telling me he died. One of our cousins. Fifty-six years old. A massive heart attack. Not wanting to believe the news, I called him immediately. The call went to voicemail. When Dwight didn't call me back or send a text message, I knew something was not right. But I was not prepared to accept that news.

This was not a cousin to whom I spoke to or saw on a regular basis, but he was always there if I needed a listening ear. And I was there for him. When we spoke, we would pick up right where we left off. We were in our twenties when we met. He thought he'd found a date, only to see me at a family reunion weeks later and find out we were related. We would always laugh about that encounter. But on this day, I felt no humor. The thought of him being gone made my heart heavy, tears flow and questions arise.

I tried so hard to make sense of his death. He died only days before his son's wedding and right before the Father's Day weekend. He would not be here for any of the celebrations. But why? I must admit I had questions for God. I didn't understand. Why did it have to be now? The timing just seemed awful. In the midst of my questioning, I was led to the Book of Proverbs. Specifically, the scripture that states, *Trust in the Lord with all thine heart and lean* not to *thine own understanding.* As I read, God spoke to my spirit, "You don't have to understand to trust."

We are so guilty of trying to figure things out. It gives us a measure of comfort to know how things work. But there are some things that we are not meant to understand, and there are other things that we don't care if we understand or not, as long as they work in our favor.

Intellectually, I cannot explain how our lungs absorb oxygen from the air, and it enters our blood and travels to our organs and body tissues to make us breathe. It really doesn't make much sense, but I don't have to understand it. All I want to do is breathe, and I trust I will.

When I think about air travel, I am told that a plane's engines are designed to move it forward at a high speed, which makes the air flow rapidly over the wings throwing air to the ground, generating an upward force that overcomes the plane's weight and holds it in the sky. I don't understand it. But if I want to go to Disney World by plane and be there in 90 minutes from the airport nearest me, as opposed to ten hours in a car, I don't have to understand it. I get on the plane and trust that it will do what it's designed to do.

When my blood pressure became elevated, while under stress some years ago, my doctor wrote a prescription in a handwriting that I could not read, to take to a pharmacist that I did not know, who gave me a small pink pill that I could not identify. I didn't understand it. But when I took the medication and my blood pressure returned to normal, I didn't care how it worked, as long as it worked. I didn't understand, but I trusted.

So, I am bothered when I hear people say they don't trust God because they don't understand. How can you trust so many human-made things but cannot trust God who is the maker of all things?

It is not logical to sit down in a chair without checking the legs or the screws to make sure it will bear your weight and not trust God who will carry your weight. It is baffling how you can get into a vehicle and drive it every day trusting that the battery, the alternator, the brakes, the transmission and the shock absorbers will work but will not trust God who gives you strength to work.

I admit I don't understand why my cousin died at the time he did, but I don't have to understand to trust. I accept and believe that God, whom I serve, makes no mistakes. His timing is perfect. Where my understanding ends, my trust begins.

Amidst my tears and the pain in my heart, that is good enough for me.

# Daily Reflections

**Pensive Moment:**

How many times have you questioned God when things did not go as you planned?

**Prayer for Today:**

*Precious Father,*
*Thank you for the conscious decision to trust You when I don't understand.*

**Daily Thoughts/Goals:**

_____

_____

_____

_____

_____

_____

_____

# Hidden in Plain Sight

He cannot read my mind
But he is in tune with my spirit

He did not journey with me
But he knows where I have been

He feels the beat of my heart
As if it were his own

I trust him with my innermost thoughts
Because he handles them with care

We are different but alike
Quiet yet courageous

He brings out the best in me
And I in him

In each other's presence the unspoken exists
But we recognize it is there

Without losing sight of each other
We focus on God and His plan

Not brought together by fate
But by Him who created us

One for the other.

# DAY 7

# Building Your Life from the Inside Out to Maximize Glory to the Lord

**Scripture Reading:**   Isaiah 43: 1-7

*Everyone who is called by My name, whom I have created for My glory: I have formed him, yes, I have made him.*   Isaiah 43:7

**Daily Devotion:**

**D**iscern who God created you to be. (Psalm 139:13-14)

**I**ncrease your knowledge of the scriptures. (2 Timothy 3:16-17)

**S**pend time with God in prayer. (1 Thessalonians 5:16-18)

**C**heerfully give and offer God your best. (2 Corinthians 9:6-7)

**I**mpart God's word into others (Matthew 28:19-20)

**P**rioritize fellowship with like-minded believers (Hebrews 10:25)

**L**ive life in a way that is worthy of the gospel (Philippians 1:27)

**I**nvoke a sense of humor (Ecclesiastes 8:15)

**N**ever give up (Galatians 6:9)

**E**mbrace humility and gratitude (James 4:10)

# Daily Reflections

**Pensive Moment:**

Building a life that is pleasing to God requires **discipline.**

**Prayer for Today:**

*Precious Father,*
*May I live with a spirit of discipline such that my life from the inside out brings maximum glory to You.*

**Daily Thoughts/Goals:**

# The Butterfly

with its strikingly frail wings of purple
and gold and yellow and red,
it pales the other insects. Delicately
sauntering from flower to flower like
a celebrity sashaying on the streets of Paris.

it's a symbol. Of resurrection,
of change and hope and life
for all to see.
Its presence delights
me as I reach out
to lay hold of the mortal creation.

the radiance of the early-morning sunshine,
the glow of the summer breeze
soaring in rhythm
with its petite-winged body
of iridescent scales in overlapping rows. Venturing
where others cannot.

running briskly alongside it
chasing it through the fields
when I finally caught it,
felt so smooth in my hands
fluttering softly in my palms.

I wanted to keep it, I am
gentle, this is life
within my hands, a miracle
of beauty I can touch
very gently. I opened my hands
and released.

(After Jorie Graham)

# DAY 8

# That Same Jesus

**Scripture Reading:** Hebrews 13:1-17

*Jesus is the same yesterday, today and forever. Hebrews 13:8*

**Daily Devotion:**

I remember the day vividly. It was September 22. Though technically the beginning of the Fall season, it was a warm day. I did one of the hardest things I have had to do as a parent. I walked with my daughter Tatum to her car as she prepared to drive to school alone. It was difficult with my son Elden, but this was my daughter. My baby. And her dad was not with us. This was supposed to be his job, not mine. I had a widow's moment, overcome with a barrage of emotions.

This would be the first time Tatum would be in the car as a licensed driver by herself. As she sat down in her vehicle, I went to the passenger side window and told my daughter to pray and to be safe. I prayed with her. I asked her to watch her surroundings and pay close attention to the actions of other drivers. I reviewed several other things with her, and then I said, "Tatum, that same Jesus who has allowed me to drive for decades without hurt or harm can do the same for you."

The book of Hebrews records that "Jesus is the same yesterday, today and forever." It means that God, in the Person of His Son Jesus, does not change. In Malachi 3:6, God affirms that "I, the Lord, do not change." His character remains the same.

- ❖ Jesus never makes promises He cannot keep.
- ❖ Jesus is even-tempered and disciplines with purpose and precision.
- ❖ Jesus is compassionate.
- ❖ Jesus is a man of truth and spoke truth wherever He went.
- ❖ Jesus is focused and persevered to complete His assignment.
- ❖ Jesus has a heart of mercy and forgiveness.

And that same Jesus – the Omniscient, Omnipotent, Omnipresent Jesus – the One who is the living water will be our water in dry places.

- ❖ That same Jesus who sent Peter to a fish to find money to pay taxes can show us how to pay our bills.
- ❖ That same Jesus who made provisions for the Widow at Zarephath can keep food on our tables.
- ❖ That same Jesus who mended the relationship between Joseph and his brothers can repair our relationships with our family members.
- ❖ That same Jesus who healed Blind Bartimaeus can give us new vision.
- ❖ That same Jesus who brought Lazarus to life can breathe life into our dead situations.
- ❖ That same Jesus who cast out demons and sent them into a herd of swine can command the evil out of us.

I sent Tatum on her way and left her in the hands of Jesus – ONE who is the same yesterday, today and forever.

# Daily Reflections

**Pensive Moment:**

Do you believe God to be a repeat offender who will bless you over and over again?

**Prayer for Today:**

*Precious Father,*
*Thank you for your consistency. For You are God who never changes.*

**Daily Thoughts/Goals:**

_____

_____

_____

_____

_____

_____

# DAY 9

# Stuck Where You Stopped

**Scripture Reading:**   Isaiah 43:1-21

*Behold, I will do a new thing, now, it shall spring forth; shall you not know it? I will even make a road in the wilderness and rivers in the desert.*
                                             Isaiah 43:19

**Daily Devotion:**

Recently, I went to the jewelers to drop off a watch that needed battery replacement. The watch had sentimental value and had been without batteries for several months. But even though the time on the watch had stopped, the time of life kept moving. The seconds, the minutes and the hours of the day kept rolling along. They didn't stop because my watch battery was dead. Life continued to happen whether the watch was working or not. Yet, on the watch, the time was frozen. It was stuck where it stopped.

Such can be the same with life. Many people find themselves stuck right where they allowed their time to stop – stuck in dead-end jobs, unfulfilling relationships and challenging situations, all because, metaphorically speaking, their batteries have stopped working. Life is passing them by. They reached a certain point, became comfortable or frustrated, and just stopped. But life doesn't stop because you decide to take time out. People will keep living and doing the things they are tasked to do whether or not you decide to participate. Sometimes, we choose to be stuck where we stopped.

Allow me to offer a few examples:

- ❖ You graduated from high school with your diploma and started working because college was not affordable. You are presented with an opportunity to continue your education, but you don't have the confidence, and you're afraid of failure. You are stuck where you stopped.

- ❖ You have a job and the only reason you go to work every day is to get paid. It offers you nothing but a means to pay your bills. Your faith is not strong enough to step out. You are stuck where you stopped.

- ❖ You were reared in the church, and you love the Lord. But your growth and understanding of God's Word have made you realize that you need more than what you're being offered where you worship. But you do nothing to change your situation. You are stuck where you stopped.

God does not want you to be stuck. The scripture states that He will make *a road in the wilderness and rivers in the desert.* God has gone before you to clear a path if you are willing to follow His directions. He has provided a means of escape. He longs to do something new in your life, but your "battery" needs replacing. You need a spiritual recharge that can only be discovered by spending time in His presence through prayer, praise and worship.

God has a plan for your life. Exploring that plan often requires taking a faithful step toward that which you cannot see to accomplish what He already knows. Only then will you conquer being stuck where you stopped.

# Daily Reflections

**Pensive Moment:**

What barriers are you allowing to keep you from fulfilling God's plan for your life?

**Prayer for Today:**

*Precious Father,*
*Thank you for recharging me spiritually, so that I may keep moving to discover what you have planned next.*

**Daily Thoughts/Goals:**

_____

_____

_____

_____

_____

_____

# DAY 10

# Good Does Not Mean Saved

**Scripture Reading:**  Romans 10:1-12

*That if you confess with your mouth the Lord Jesus and believe in your heart that God has raised Him from the dead, you will be saved. For with the heart, one believes unto righteous, and with the mouth, confession is made unto salvation.* Romans 10: 9-10

**Daily Devotion:**

Thanksgiving Day in the United States is observed officially on the fourth Thursday of November each year. In addition to the traditional feasts of all kinds of foods, there is a spirit of giving and helping others. Homeless people enjoy meals that they don't receive at other times of the year; churches collect canned goods and prepare gift boxes to distribute to families in need. Monies are sent across continents to sponsor children who live in impoverished areas. These are all good works that bring joy to the recipients. But we must remember in the context of Christianity, good works are not the basis for salvation.

Over the course of my life, I have observed pastors masterfully eulogize people who demonstrated no evidence of acknowledging Jesus as their Personal Savior. Yet, in an attempt to comfort grieving families, these eulogists would speak about the good deeds performed by the deceased. They would talk about personal character traits like integrity, kindness and humility. And somewhere toward the end of the eulogy, language was inserted to provide the family comfort that their loved one would live eternally with Jesus. But would they?

While only God knows the condition of one's heart, the Bible states in Romans 10:9 that salvation is contingent upon confessing with your mouth the Lord Jesus and believing in your heart that God raised Jesus from the dead. But oftentimes, people equate salvation with good works. Though it is admirable to do good works, which have their proper places in the life of a Christian, good works do not produce salvation.

Salvation produces good works because the saved person desires to reflect the character and the goodness of the Savior. Before we are saved, nothing that we do pleases God. Therefore, as Christians, we perform good works not to be saved but because we are saved. Having faith in Jesus Christ is the hallmark of being a Christian, and the good works thereafter serve as evidence of salvation.

# Daily Reflections

**Pensive Moment:**

In what ways are you trying to work your way into God's Kingdom?

**Prayer for Today:**

*Precious Father,*
*Thank you for salvation. I bless you for the works that follow.*

**Daily Thoughts/Goals:**

_____

_____

_____

_____

_____

_____

# Zuihitsu Poetry

The most dangerous place in the world to be is the place where no one can tell you anything. A fool will listen only to himself.

Sap cascading the black olive tree is reminiscent of hot wax oozing down scented votive candles.

I wouldn't trade a thing for the knowledge I've gained or the lessons I've learned like appreciating every moment. The trip has made me stronger, wiser and better.

The whirs of the tornadic winds pounding upon the chestnut doors of the stable were a reminder that life could end without warning.

Finish what you start – no one wins a 400-meter race by stopping in the middle of a lap or looking around to assess the applause of the crowd.

The extent to which we travel to impress others is not worth the distance of the journey.

My happiness is not predicated upon the favorability of my circumstances.

I have real joy.

# Retirement

Entering the crowded lecture hall
Dried crusty tears stained my face.

Vague memories of a distinguished career.

Colleagues who once acknowledged
My intellect   my elegance   my grace

Now look upon me with solace.

A three-car accident that murky afternoon
Changed my life forever.

From walking to rolling – disfigured and wheelchair-bound.

Deep breaths I take while mimicking a smile
A celebration to honor me.

Forced retirement.

# DAY 11

# All Means Everyone

**Scripture Reading:**     Romans 3:21-26

*For all have sinned and fall short of the glory of God.*  Romans 3:23

**Daily Devotion:**

I was extremely blessed to begin a relationship with Jesus at an early age. I was saved when I was 11 years old, and while the saints at my home church referred to salvation as "joining the church," even I knew there was more to my action. I wanted a personal connection to Jesus, and I was willing to place my faith and trust in Him.

Though I was a child and spoke like a child, and behaved as a child does, I knew there was something different about my life that was far from childlike. I was excited about going to church, and I enjoyed sitting on the front pew during revival. I chose to attend the University of North Carolina at Chapel Hill, in part, because it was close enough for me to come home every weekend for our church worship service. Among other things, I served as an usher and did not want to miss the opportunity to be one of the first greeters at the church door.

When the sanctuary doors opened, I was there. I grew up in church, but more importantly, church grew up in me. I believed Jesus to be my friend, and as a child, I never felt like I was not saved. But being saved is not about a feeling. Many people have made an emotional confession of salvation, only to discover later that they were caught up in the moment, whatever that moment entailed for them. When I accepted Jesus Christ into my life, I was filled with emotion but completely aware of the commitment I was making.

Receiving Christ as Personal Savior is making a conscious choice to give your life to Jesus because you know you are a sinner in need of forgiveness for your sins. God caught me early before I knew what I didn't know. I used to hear the testimonies of the senior saints about being a "wretch" and doing everything they were big and bad enough to do. But at age 11, I couldn't say I was a wretch because I had no idea what a wretch was, and I wasn't big enough to be bad enough to do much.

Because I accepted Christ early, I went from the safety of my parents' care to the safety of God's care with the appearance of minimal transition. But there was indeed a transition. There was a turning point in my life. Though I did not have the vocabulary to fully explain my experience, I know now that when the revival preacher, Dr. Cardes H. Brown Jr., extended the invitation for me to give my life to Christ, on July 29, 1974, something happened when I accepted Jesus. I surrendered the sinful life I was born into - the sinful ways that would attempt to overtake me. I accepted the gift of God's salvation and the beauty of His grace.

Whether we receive salvation early or later in life, we all sin and fall short of the glory of God. Without distinction, each of us is deserving of the wrath of God for the sin that lies within us – both public and private. We have a sinful nature, and we must die to sin daily. God, through His Son Jesus, has given us a means of escape from the penalty of sin. When we confess our sins and accept Jesus as Lord through our faith, we are justified, that is, placed in right standing with God, our Father.

I was not the typical young person, and you may not have been either, but we don't have to see sin to know it exists because the Bible tells us so. Until we accept Christ as our Savior, we are all sinners. All means everyone, and everyone means you and me.

# Daily Reflections

**Pensive Moment:**

Do you remember the time you said, *"yes"*, to the Lord's invitation?

**Prayer for Today:**

*Precious Father,*
*Thank you for saving a sinner like me. Help me to declare to the entire world that salvation is free.*

**Daily Thoughts/Goals:**

_____

_____

_____

_____

_____

_____

# DAY 12

# You're Under Consideration

**Scripture Reading:**   Job 1:6-22

*And the Lord said to Satan, "From where you come?" So, Satan answered the Lord and said, "From going to and fro on the earth, and from walking back and forth on it." Then the Lord said to Satan, "Have you considered My servant Job, that there is none like him on the earth, a blameless and upright man, one who fears God and shuns evil?"* Job 1:7-8

**Daily Devotion:**

Having spent much of my career in human resources, I reviewed applications for employment, matching the applicants' qualifications alongside the responsibilities of vacant positions. After submitting their credentials, applicants would contact the human resources department asking if their applications had been reviewed and if they were under consideration for a job. On numerous occasions, I responded affirmatively to that question, but at other times, I had to tell the applicant that their application was no longer being considered.

In our scripture, but speaking metaphorically, we are privy to a meeting with the human resources director in Heaven – One who is in charge of reviewing all candidates. On this day, in the conclave of the heavenly court, it is where He, The Lord, presides. The sons of God have come to present themselves before the Lord, and Satan was permitted to attend. In this meeting, a man named Job was introduced into the equation. He was an upright man, the spiritual leader and the priest of his household. He was extremely wealthy, married with ten children and owned thousands of livestock. He was blameless and stayed away from evil.

As the Lord talked to Satan during this meeting, He asked him what he had been doing. Satan responded that he has been moving about on the earth and walking up and down. God asked Satan, "Have you considered my servant Job?" Simply put, God was asking Satan if Job would be a suitable candidate for what he was looking for? Satan responded to the Lord by suggesting that it was his understanding that the Lord had placed a hedge of protection around Job and blessed the work of his hands. And Satan was correct. However, knowing that Job's faith was real and that he would pass any test, the Lord agreed to remove the protection and placed all that Job had in Satan's hands, with the understanding that Satan could not lay a hand upon Job's soul. Thereby, Job was under consideration for a job for which he had not applied.

Satan began his work, afflicting Job by killing his children, destroying his livelihood, ruining his health, and causing his wife to declare that he should curse God and die – all because God placed Job under consideration. It was God's idea. And to no surprise to God, Job prevailed. He bore his trials patiently and charged God with no wrongdoing.

If you have ever been presented with a challenge, or a set of debilitating circumstances, that you did not cause, consider that God has placed you under consideration. It is God who mentioned your name to Satan. But Satan's power is limited by God's control. Satan believes that you will succumb under the pressure he applies, but God knows you will prevail. He allows the test to show you that your faith is genuine, and it has the strength to overcome. God tests your faith to produce patience, so that you will become spiritually mature and complete.

God has you on His mind, and His tests confirm that you are under consideration.

# Daily Reflections

**Pensive Moment:**

*Have you ever had a difficult situation that made you doubt the sovereignty of God?*

**Prayer for Today:**

*Precious Father,*
*Thank you for helping me to realize that my faith is real.*

**Daily Thoughts/Goals:**

_____

_____

_____

_____

_____

_____

# DAY 13

# Mother, Where Art Thou?

**Scripture Reading:**  Luke 15:11-32

*And he arose and came to his father. But when he was still a great way off, his father saw him and had compassion and ran and fell on his neck and kissed him.*  Luke 15:20

**Daily Devotion:**

The Parable of the Prodigal Son is one of the most well-known parables in the Bible. It tells the story of a man who had two sons – the younger son wanted his inheritance from his father, which he goes out and spends on riotous living. When his money disappears so do his friends and his livelihood. He reaches such a low point that he sells himself into slavery, feeds pigs and even desires to eat the cornhusks fed to the animals. He begged, but no one would give him anything. He is reduced to nothing. It is at this lowest point in his life that he comes to his senses, returns home to his father and confesses his sins. The father greets him with open arms, gives him food, provides him with a robe and places sandals on his feet and a beautiful ring on his finger. The relationship is restored.

This parable seeks to make the point that God will allow the sinner to go their own way, but if the sinner returns and repents, the same God that allowed them to go in the first place will allow them to come back and will receive them with open arms. But at first read, the new bible student may not glean the meaning of this parable and the importance of being able to return home to your father when, in your human frailty, you make costly mistakes.

As I have read this parable over the years, I have pondered why there is no mention of the prodigal son's mother. The scripture opens with, *"Then He said, a certain man had two sons."* No reference to the mother. But at some point, she existed. She carried this son growing in her body. Where she went, he went. What she ate, he ate. In the most private moments of her day, he was there. When she spoke, he heard it; when she laughed, he felt the vibration; when she cried, he sobbed. And yet, when he returned home, she was not present. It makes you wonder if she was alive when he left home. If so, can you imagine the heartbreak she felt when her baby boy took to the streets with more dollars than sense, thinking life owed him something, and he had it all together?

Imaginatively speaking, she stayed up and walked the premises of their home, rubbed, and twisted her hands while she prayed. Petitioned angels to be a hedge of protection around her son both day and night – lying down to sleep only to be awakened by what she perceived to be sounds of his cries that she could not soothe.

She had no mobile device to call him. No internet. No social media. No location-based services. The anguish she must have experienced knowing that she fed him from her breast when he was hungry; doctored him when he was sick; counseled him when he was confused. And yet, when he returned home, she was not there. Mother, where art thou? The scripture does not tell us, but every mother who has a child who has gone astray believes, just like the prodigal son's mother, they will come back again. And not just to the mother and the family but to the Father – the Heavenly Father – the forgiving One and the Restorer of broken fellowship.

# Daily Reflections

**Pensive Moment:**

Are you willing to forgive and embrace those you love when they come back home?

**Prayer for Today:**

*Precious Father,*
*Thank you for bringing me home again, not just to my family but to You, so that I may be restored.*

**Daily Thoughts/Goals:**

_____

_____

_____

_____

_____

_____

# And Baby Needs a Pair of Shoes

Two decades of memories
In one dusty trunk
On the cold, cracked basement floor –
My grandmother's house.

Blue willow tea sets
Julia Barbie doll – the only black one
Tonka toys, finger painting, royal blue papier-mache'
With clumpy glue

All over my hands.

Sweaty field day, a stained faded ribbon
Middle school dance, a crumbled carnation
He kissed me with one lip.

So awkward.

High school was bewildering –
Parallel parking, debate team matches, scholastic exams
Falling in love for the very first time
With clammy palms and trembling hands.

College introduced new liberties –
Late night parties, tailgating, pepperoni pizza
Delivered to the door.
Stresses far and few.

Fun is over now.

Adult life emerges
Bills become my norm –
Student loans, mobile devices, mortgages, groceries
And baby needs a pair of shoes.

# Haiku Sonnet

Succulent and warm
peach cobbler pacifies the taste buds
and delights the soul.

Relaxing and cool
the fall breeze filled the sunroom
like gas fills a tank.

Believing our God
she prayed with faith and power
that a change would come

He stood mortified
accepting accusations
without any guilt.

Postponed pain
extends torture.

# DAY 14

# Is That Your Final Answer?

**Scripture Reading:**   Luke 18: 1-8

*And he would not for a while; but afterward, he said within himself, 'Though I do not fear God nor regard man, yet because this widow troubles me, I will avenge her, lest by her continual coming she weary me.'*
Luke 18: 4-5

**Daily Devotion:**

On the popular television game show "*Who Wants to be a Millionaire*," the late Regis Philbin created dramatic tension in every episode of the show as he asked each contestant upon hearing their response to a question, "Is that your final answer?" In doing so, he gave the contestant an opportunity to change their mind.

In Luke 18, we are introduced to a persistent widow who has come into contact with an unjust judge – one who did not fear God and did not respect man. This widow kept coming to this judge asking him to give her justice against her adversary, a power that only the judge had. The scripture states that she kept coming, and he kept refusing to grant her petition. But that did not stop her from asking repeatedly. I can imagine that the widow said to the judge, "Is that your final answer?" The judge eventually gave in and said, even though I do not fear God, nor do I respect man, I will give her justice, so she will not continually wear me down.

In the case of this widow, God answered her request because her continued petition demonstrated the longing for what she was asking, and He promised justice for her. God does not always give us what we want when we want it, but it is beneficial to keep asking.

The Bible states in Psalm 34:7, *"Delight thyself in the Lord, and He will give thee the desires of thine heart."* If we are willing to receive and listen to God with our spirit, He will place within our hearts the desires that He wishes us to have. Desires that line up with His Will come to pass. His Will is revealed in His Word – the Bible.

Christians should pray always and not lose heart. When God does not respond affirmatively to our requests, it is one of three reasons: we are not asking in accordance with His Will; we are asking outside of His Timing, or He is creating within us patience and perseverance. Until God says "no" or removes the desires from our hearts, we should keep asking, "Is that your final answer?"

# Daily Reflections

**Pensive Moment:**

Do you ever become weary in your petitions when you don't see God move on your behalf?

**Prayer for Today:**

*Precious Father,*
*I praise You for persistence and thank you for patience, as I await your response.*

**Daily Thoughts/Goals:**

_____

_____

_____

_____

_____

_____

# DAY 15

# I'll Make Room for Jesus

**Scripture Reading:**   Luke 2: 1-20

*And she brought forth her firstborn Son and wrapped Him in swaddling clothes and laid Him in a manger because there was no room for them in the inn.*  Luke 2:7

**Daily Devotion:**

The Bible records the birth of Jesus in the Book of Luke and also in the Book of Matthew. Christians refer to this narrative as The Christmas Story.

It begins with a decree ordered by Emperor Caesar Augustus requiring everyone in the Roman territory to be registered in their hometown for the purposes of taxation. This meant that Joseph, being from the house and the family lineage of David, would travel from his home in Nazareth to the City of Bethlehem. Mary was pregnant and almost ready to deliver. Yet, she had to travel with Joseph. The journey was believed to be about 90 miles.

While in Bethlehem, the time came for Mary to have her baby. With the number of people returning to the city to be counted, there were no rooms available for them in the inn. No place for this family. So, Mary, the mother of the baby who would become the Savior of the world, resorted to having her baby Jesus in meager accommodations in a place where animals were believed to be kept. He was laid in a manger, a feeding trough for animals. The King of all creation, the Lord of Lords, the Alpha and Omega, who deserved all honor and glory, was born into the humblest of circumstances.

Over 2000 years ago, when Jesus made entry into this world, there was no room for him in the inn. And 2000 years later, for some, not much has changed. They have made no room for Jesus. But He does not seek a place in our house. Jesus seeks a place in our hearts.

- ☐ We make room for Jesus because his birth is good news – an event met with joy and good news for all people.
- ☐ We make room for Jesus because He is the Savior who delivered us from sin, took the sting out of death and provided us with a glorious opportunity of eternal life.
- ☐ We make room for Jesus because He is the Messiah who fulfills the Law and the Prophets – physically accomplishing all that the scriptures said He would and yet making plain through His teachings the proclamation of His Word.
- ☐ We make room for Jesus because He is the Divine Lord of all things who took on human flesh to identify with us, His creation.
- ☐ We make room for Jesus because he is the RESCUER in the drama triangle who saved us from a life of hopelessness to a life of helpfulness as He gently knocks on the door of our hearts waiting for an invitation to come in.
- ☐ We make room for Jesus because there would be no life without Him.

# Daily Reflections

**Pensive Moment:**

What is occupying space in your life such that you have no room for Jesus?

**Prayer for Today:**

*Precious Father,
I welcome you into my heart today. I have room for you.*

**Daily Thoughts/Goals:**

_____

_____

_____

_____

_____

_____

# DAY 16

# The Holy Spirit Sensor

**Scripture Reading:**   Matthew 11:25-29

*Come to Me, all you who labor and are heavy laden, and I will give you rest.* Matthew 11:28

**Daily Devotion:**

Appliance shopping is one of my least favorite things to do, so I was less than elated when I had to purchase a washing machine. Deciding on a top loader as opposed to a front loader, efficiency, noise level and size were all things I considered. It was a tedious task.

The new machines have sensors for everything – water level sensors, temperature sensors, load balance sensors, door lock sensors and detergent dispenser sensors. Apparently, these sensors function to make sure the washing process is safe, efficient and effective. When a malfunction occurs with the machine, the sensor is the first to provide an alert.

I was particularly intrigued by the load balance sensor. It's a vibration sensor that detects the movement of the machine drum. If the load is unbalanced, meaning too many clothes are on one side or the other, the sensor will send a signal to the control board. As a result, the spin cycle adjusts itself and redistributes the load, which keeps the washing machine from breaking. In rare cases, clothes may have to be removed from the machine if too many have been added. But the sensor provides an alert when a load is too heavy.

How the sensor sends signals to the washing machine made me think about life as a Christian. Oftentimes, we carry loads that are in excess of what we need to bear. We are weighed down by financial mishaps that leave us with little savings and living paycheck to paycheck. We have problems with our relationships, exposing cracks in our foundation which cause moisture and mildew of our biological connections. We struggle with health maladies that are complicated and expensive to treat. All these loads can potentially weaken our faith. Sometimes we are so heavy-laden with the cares of a fallen world that the weight shows in our gait - the way we move and live and have our being. Our physical and spiritual dispositions become clearly visible for all to see - evidence that there is a problem with the load.

However, we should remember that when we accepted Jesus Christ as our Personal Savior, God gave us a sensor, much like that in the washing machine. Our sensor is the Holy Spirit, who takes up residence in our hearts when we become saved. This God-given mechanism acts as our Helper, our Comforter and our Guide. Because Jesus had to leave us physically, He left the Holy Spirit to guide us to all truth, go before us, lead the way and help us to handle the obstacles of life. When our loads become heavy and get out of balance, the Holy Spirit speaks to our hearts and our minds to let us know that we are carrying too much – that we need to release our cares and concerns to Jesus to help us rebalance.

Jesus wants to help. He extends the invitation for us to come to him when we are weary and heavy with burdens.

- ☐ Jesus will be a dolly to help us carry concerns that are too heavy for us.

- ☐ Jesus will be castors on the bottom of the load, so we can roll it.

- ☐ Jesus will be gliders to help slide issues around from the place they are to the place they need to be.

Whatever we need, Jesus will be that, if we adhere to the sensor of the Holy Spirit and take all things to Him in prayer.

# Daily Reflections

**Pensive Moment:**

What are you carrying that you need to release?

**Prayer for Today:**

*Precious Father,*
*I am grateful for my new heart and the Holy Spirit that helps me to hear and to obey even when it is not convenient.*

**Daily Thoughts/Goals:**

_____

_____

_____

_____

_____

_____

# DAY 17

# Make Room to Learn

**Scripture Reading:**    Proverbs 1:1-7

*The fear of the Lord is the beginning of knowledge, but fools despise wisdom and instruction.* Proverbs 1:7

**Daily Devotion:**

When my daughter went to preschool, her teacher's motto was "Learn, learn, learn." "Miss Frances," as she was known by her students, was lovingly strict and had high expectations. She instilled in them the value of learning, even at their young ages, and she taught them well. All her students were ready to go to kindergarten after graduating from preschool. My daughter was prepared to go to kindergarten a year early.

Most people will agree that education is important. Minimally, it shows what we have the ability to accomplish, the value of hard work and the need for growth and development – all important components of being better and informed citizens in our communities.

While college may not be a desire or a need for everyone, learning should be a priority. Failing to learn can make you feel lost, isolated, and disconnected. Generally speaking, we don't like what we don't know how to do, and many times, we don't know how because we refuse to learn.

While Christian education is not specifically mentioned in scripture, it is implied throughout the Bible. There are a multitude of references made to instruction, knowledge and wisdom. A few include:

- Proverbs 18:15 – *"The heart of the prudent acquires knowledge, and the ear of the wise seeks knowledge."*
- 2 Timothy 3:16 – *"All scripture is given by inspiration of God, and is profitable for doctrine, for reproof, for correction, for instruction in righteousness."*
- Philippians 4:9 - *"The things which you learned and received and heard and saw in me, these do, and the God of peace will be with you."*

During the pandemic, most of us were given tremendous opportunities to learn. Our bedrooms became offices; the living rooms were places of worship, and the dining room tables doubled as desks while parents became homeschool teachers. The unwelcome pandemic lockdown provided a time of family connection and self-reflection. You can learn a lot when you're grounded.

- Some learned that if they did not have to go out to work, they'd stay in pajamas all day long – no shower, no teeth brushed, no hair combed, no motivation. Others appreciated not having to leave home so much that they worked harder at their home office.
- Some learned that they don't know how to manage their time without a supervisor. Others learned they work more efficiently in the absence of supervision because all time belongs to God.
- Some learned that the pandemic provided a great excuse to forsake the assembling of ourselves together. Others learned the importance of coming together as a united body of Christ.

Whatever you learn, it is important to keep learning. Though many life events, like the pandemic, are tragic, there is always a lesson to learn. Only a fool rejects knowledge.

# Daily Reflections

**Pensive Moment:**

What roadblocks, in life, need to be removed to clear the path for your spiritual growth?

**Prayer for Today:**

*Precious Father,*
*Give me a desire to stretch my mind beyond what makes me comfortable so that I may learn.*

**Daily Thoughts/Goals:**

_____

_____

_____

_____

_____

_____

_____

# DAY 18

# God Always Has a Batter on Deck

**Scripture Reading:** Joshua 1:1-19

*After the death of Moses, the servant of the Lord, it came to pass that the Lord spoke to Joshua the son of Nun, Moses' assistant, saying, 'Moses My servant is dead. Now therefore, arise, go over this Jordan, you and all this people, to the land which I am giving to them – the children of Israel. Every place that the sole of your foot will tread upon I have given you, as I said to Moses.* Joshua 1:1-3

**Daily Devotion:**

In the game of baseball, "on deck" refers to being the next in line to go to the plate to bat. The batter on deck must be watchful and prepared, as being on deck guarantees a chance at bat if certain situations take place. The on-deck batter comes after the batter at the plate. But the game of baseball is not the only place where there is a batter on deck. God always has a batter on deck – that is, someone prepared to go next.

We know from our Bible reading that Moses was tasked with leading the children of Israel out of Egypt and toward The Promised Land. God provided Moses with specific instructions. His brother Aaron accompanied him. The Israelites wandered for 40 years, but towards the end of their journey, they approached a desert. There was no water. God told Moses and his brother Aaron what to do to bring forth water. Moses was to speak to the rock in the desert and tell it to yield water. Instead, Moses hit the rock. While water came forth, those were not God's instructions on this occasion. Moses decided to follow his own plan. This angered God because Moses was disloyal to Him in the presence of the Israelites. He failed to follow God's command. As a result, God told Moses, along with Aaron, that they would not be allowed to take the Israelites to The Promised Land, nor would they be permitted to enter. Moses died. God needed someone to complete the assignment.

Without any pause or hesitation, God commissioned Joshua, the son of Nun and the second in command to Moses. God did not advertise the position. He did not accept applications. He did not review resumes. He did not conduct interviews. He simply gave Joshua instructions. God already had a batter on deck.

God told Joshua that his servant Moses was dead, and He wanted Joshua to cross the Jordan and take His people to the land that He had promised. God further told Joshua that everywhere his foot tread would belong to him and that he need not worry about anything because he would never leave him nor forsake him. In other words, God made Joshua invincible and promised him that victory was imminent. Joshua was victorious.

God always has a successor prepared – one who will follow His instructions. Joshua was not the only batter on deck in the Bible. Elijah was about to come to the end of his prophetic journey when God spoke to him and told him to commission Elisha. Elisha had been in training with Elijah for years, and he was prepared to succeed Elijah. He was waiting on deck for his turn at bat. When Elijah came by and cast his cloak upon the young man, Elisha recognized the gesture as a transfer of authority, and he positioned himself to follow the command.

When Adam and Eve were playing the blame game in the Garden at home plate and did not carry out the assignment set forth by God, Jesus was waiting on deck. Tasked to shoulder the burdens and the sins of the entire world, Jesus made sure that God's Perfect Will was executed and that every tongue that confessed, *Jesus is Lord*, would get a chance to go home.

Christians should follow God's example of preparation. Does your family have a succession plan? Have you shared the gospel of Jesus Christ with those whom you will leave behind? When you close your eyes in death, will you leave money, cars, houses, land or will you leave the legacy of a saved generation — somebody waiting on deck to carry out the mission of kingdom-building? Who do you have in training such that the Word of God can strengthen them? Are you simply trying to make it to first base without any concern for what happens next? Are you a heavy spiritual hitter who makes others get excited about coming after you, or are you comfortable getting by with a "walk," preserving only what benefits you? All questions a Christian should ponder.

Joshua succeeded Moses with success; Elisha succeeded Elijah with triumph. Jesus stepped to the plate to remedy the chaos created by Adam and Eve. Who will succeed you? Who is on deck in your life waiting to get a turn at bat?

# Daily Reflections

**Pensive Moment:**

In what ways is God preparing you for your next assignment?

**Prayer for Today:**

*Precious Father,*
*Allow me to live so that those who follow will want to continue the assignment of building up your kingdom.*

**Daily Thoughts/Goals:**

# Daybreak

as the crust on my eyelashes
cracks open to the blessings
of a day I've never witnessed before
I hear the waves pounding the rocky seashore
smell the bourbon bacon at the surfside grill
and embrace the radiant glow
of God's brightest morning star
beaming through the bedroom window
like a shiny silver dollar
at the base of Roman's Trevi Fountain

# DAY 19

# Go and Sin No More

**Scripture Reading:**   John 8: 1-12

*Then the scribes and Pharisees brought to Him a woman caught in adultery. And when they had set her in the midst, they said to Him, 'Teacher, this woman was caught in adultery, in the very act.* John 8:3-4

**Daily Devotion:**

In the Book of John, the scribes and the Pharisees have brought a woman to Jesus who has been caught in adultery. Within this text lies a smorgasbord of teaching principles that can be examined and discussed.

- ❖ We can talk about how the scribes and the Pharisees were trying to trap Jesus. The Mosaic Law required that the woman be stoned for her sin. If Jesus opposed her death, He was opposing the Law of Moses. Yet, if Jesus advocated her death, an issue would arise with the Romans because Jews, under Roman rule, were not permitted to carry out their own executions.
- ❖ We can talk about how the scribes and the Pharisees brought the woman to Jesus, and not the man. If the woman was caught in adultery, so was the man. The Law of Moses maintained that both the man and the woman be judged.
- ❖ We can talk about how these accusers, who were men, took this woman to Jesus while they were grappling with their own sins.

However, I choose to direct your attention to what Jesus did and said in response to this woman being brought before Him. As He listened to the charges of adultery being lodged against her, Jesus knelt on the ground and began writing in the dirt with his finger. The scriptures do not expound upon what He wrote. As the accusers continued to level the charges, Jesus stood up and He replied, *"He that is without sin among you, let him throw a stone at her first."* Then Jesus stooped down on the ground a second time and once again began to write. The Bible tells us that as He did, one by one, every scribe and every Pharisee walked away having been convicted by their own conscience. Jesus stood up again, being alone with the woman, and asked her, *"Woman where are those accusers of yours? Has no one condemned you?"* She said, *"No one, Lord."* Jesus said, *"Neither do I condemn you; go and sin no more."* (John 8: 7-11)

The question that is reasonable to ponder is, "Why did Jesus let the woman go without apparent punishment and knowing that humans sin, why did he tell her to sin no more?" Let me offer some contextual clarification.

This woman was guilty. The Bible says that she was caught in the act. But the people who were exposing her sin – putting her name on social media, sending group text messages, and trying to schedule a meeting with her pastor – had their own sins to contend with. They were pointing out the sins of this woman without considering their own sins. Jesus spoke clearly and did not stutter when He told the accusers whomever was blameless could be the first one in line to stone this woman. The scripture states they all walked away, having recognized their own sinful ways.

In addition to the woman being culpable, she came into contact with Jesus. Yes, she was brought to Jesus, but she made contact. And the scripture states that when she addressed Him, she referred to Jesus as Lord. She knew who He was.

You cannot come into contact with Jesus, recognize the Sovereignty of who He is and remain the same. Connecting with Jesus gave this woman a fresh perspective on the life she was living, so the Lord did only one thing, and that was to tell her to "GO AND SIN NO MORE." He wasn't dismissing the fact that she was guilty or excusing her adulterous ways. He wasn't saying woman you are now without any sin. His actions and His words communicated that because she met Him, her life had been changed and the appeal that sin had was now gone. This woman had a close encounter of the third kind. When she met Jesus, she was introduced to the Father. She was introduced to the Son. She was introduced to the Holy Spirit. Her life would never be the same. Jesus extended to this woman His grace and His mercy.

Every Christian's desire should be to sin no more. When you meet and accept Jesus, your desires will shift from your flesh to His Will. Your former ways may tug at you and attempt to pull you back in, but your desires have changed. And if you still long after the things that are carnal, check your internet router for interference that may have weakened your signal or caused you to lose connection to your spiritual source of power.

There is a difference between making a mistake and choosing to live a lifestyle of sin. When we choose sin as a lifestyle, we are consciously acting outside the Will of God knowing that our choices are not honoring His Word. God loves His children and offers us His grace and His mercy. Any sin that we commit should be accidental and not intentional.

# Daily Reflections

**Pensive Moment:**

Think about a time when you deserved punishment, but God said, *"Go and sin no more."*

**Prayer for Today:**

*Precious Father,*
*Plant within me the desires of my heart that will honor Your Word instead of my flesh.*

**Daily Thoughts/Goals:**

_____

_____

_____

_____

_____

_____

# Fairview Neighborhood

Sometimes I wish I were on the cracked concrete porch with grandma singing the Negro spirituals of how we got over and waiting for the streetlight to come on as the sun hides behind the summer evening clouds.

Sometimes I wish daddy would walk through the heavy wooden door of the little green house with his gray hunting pants chock-full of rabbits so I could pull one out of each blood-stained pocket.

Sometimes I wish I could run across the graveled dusty road to Hattie Lee Brown's house and interrupt her soap operas to get my favorite Fifth Avenue chocolate bar from her paperboard box filled with sugary treats.

Sometimes I wish I could see Granny Wilson strolling through Mable Wade's backyard with a pan of homemade buttered yeast rolls covered with a floral drying towel.

Sometimes I wish living life didn't mean losing things you love so much.

Sometimes I wish I could taste my mother's delicious chicken 'n dumplins' made the ol' fashioned way with homemade dough pressed with a rolling pin.

Sometimes I wish I could see Osea Rainey in her plaid dress standing in the corner and talking for hours because she thought it was something magical about our house.

Sometimes I wish I could braid the long silky hair of Julia Wilson and see her daughter Annie Mae laughing and coughing as she puffs on her cigarettes.

Sometimes I wish I could hear the gray tin box on the front porch closing as the milk man brings fresh chocolate milk.

Sometimes I wish I could see Fluffy spinning in circles and barking as he chases his black and white whip tail.

*Anna Neal — I never wished — BUT! I'm glad God blessed me with a friend I can sit next to on a bench and be seeing. I love you — Linda Faye, July 2024*

# DAY 20

# Constructed with Success in Mind

**Scripture Reading:**   Psalm 127

*Unless the Lord builds the house, they labor in vain who build it.*
Psalm 127:1a

**Daily Devotion:**

A crucial factor in the building of a house is selecting the contractor. The contractor has the responsibility of planning and overseeing the construction activities so that the project is completed in a timely fashion and within the budget.

Most of us have witnessed the start of projects and watched them halted, and in some cases, never finished. Reasons such as insufficient labor, lack of resources and absence of funds can stall a building project. It is the job of the contractor to make sure that everything is on schedule, obligations are met, funds are available, and the project is finished to completion.

For the Christian, building a life is very much like building a house. It requires a good contractor for the project to be successful. Though it gives us a measure of comfort, satisfaction and power to think our life is our own, it is not. When you accept Christ as your Personal Savior, you are surrendering your will to His Will with the understanding that your life is no longer yours to do as you please. Your contractor has been sovereignly selected. His name is Jesus, and He will be with you throughout the construction.

When you make a covenant with God and His Son Jesus, you trust Him to build your life, according to His plans, the way He sees fit – believing that it will work for your good. And while God gives you freedom to choose, accepting Him as Savior makes the statement that you have chosen Him. It is a surrender that allows God to take the wheel of your life and be the chauffeur of your destiny.

In Psalm 127, King Solomon, the wisest and richest man to ever live, unequivocally states that life without God as the foundation is meaningless, senseless and without value. He understood the relevance of life with God and the importance of following His plans.

- ❖ God gave Noah specific plans, and his family was spared from the flood.
- ❖ God had plans for Abraham to be the Father of all Nations, and Abraham succeeded.
- ❖ God led Moses to the parting of the Red Sea, so the Israelites could walk across on dry land. Nobody got wet.
- ❖ God was present when Jesus turned water into wine at the wedding feast and impressed the host.

Wherever God is there is victory. But failing to have Him draw up your plans and function as your Contractor leads to a botched building. If God is not a part of your blueprint for life, nothing you do has value.

Your spiritual house should be built with wisdom and established through understanding such that each of the rooms is filled with the fruit of the spirit – love, joy, peace, patience, kindness, goodness, gentleness, faithfulness and self-control.

You can have plans, but God has *purpose*.

# Daily Reflections

**Pensive Moment:**

What are you working on that does not have God as part of the plan?

**Prayer for Today:**

*Precious Father,*
*Please show me how to yield to the plan and the purpose that you have for my life.*

**Daily Thoughts/Goals:**

_____

_____

_____

_____

_____

# DAY 21

# Set Up for Victory

**Scripture Reading:**   1 Corinthians 15:50-57

*But thanks be to God, who gives us the victory through our Lord Jesus Christ.* 1 Corinthians 15:57

**Daily Devotion:**

In the 1970s, with only three major networks and a few local channels, watching television was certainly not as entertaining as it is now with streaming services and hundreds of program choices. Yet, it was a pastime activity that I really enjoyed.

Every Saturday night, my sister and I watched professional wrestling with our dad. I remember vividly wrestlers Wahoo McDaniel, Rick Flair, Paul Jones, Ricky Steamboat, Blackjack Mulligan, and the famous Rufus R. "Freight Train" Jones. We would yell and scream at the television, cheering on our favorite wrestler as if our heightened emotions would somehow affect the outcome of the match. It was only years later we realized that professional wrestling was a form of athletic theater for the purposes of entertainment.

Though elements of skill and athletics were necessary, the wrestling matches, that I watched as a kid, were not in the category of competitive sports. The wrestlers were entertainers paid to please the crowd. The stunts were scripted, and the outcomes of the matches were predetermined. It looked so real on television, but one in-person visit was proof enough that the events were staged, and the winner declared before the match began. The designated winner had one job and that was to make the theater performance look convincing. They stepped into the ring, backed into a corner, took a few body slams into the ropes or onto the mat and walked away with victory because the match was fixed.

The life of a Christian has some similarities to that of a professional wrestler. Metaphorically speaking, the challenges and trials that we face are reminiscent of being inside a ring with an opponent. And while the opponent looks formidable, we are aware that we have been promised victory. The Word of God declares that we win.

Throughout the Bible are countless examples of winners – people who stepped into the ring of adversity and won. They were destitute, misunderstood, mistreated and abused. They were battered and often bruised. But they won!

- ❖ Joseph, the eleventh son of Jacob, was hated and sold into slavery by his brothers because they were jealous. He was accused of sexual assault that he did not commit and placed in jail. But his setup played out in victory. He became a ruler in Egypt, second only to the king. This assignment positioned him to provide food for his father and his brothers during a famine in the land.

- ❖ Ruth, a woman of Moab who married the son of an Israelite family, became widowed. She sacrificed her own comfort to care for her mother-in-law Naomi, who introduced her to the God of Israel. Ruth gleaned in the fields of a place that was not her home, so they could have food. It was there she met her kinsman redeemer, the male relative in her late husband's family who had the responsibility to rescue or help the widow in need. The connection to this man named Boaz resulted in marriage with Ruth giving birth to a child and blessing her to be in the lineage of Jesus.

Joseph and Ruth were set up to be winners.

Nobody has to convince the designated winner of a wrestling match that they won. They know the victory is theirs because the promise has been made – the deal sealed beforehand.

It doesn't matter how close Christians come to being counted out, we win! When Jesus died on the cross for the propitiation of our sins, the promise was made. How comforting it is to know that when we are backed into a corner, slammed against the ropes or thrown onto the mat, we still win. When the referee concludes the countdown, he will lift our hands in victory no matter what the situation looks like. We must arise from our mats knowing that everything we endure as Christians is orchestrated by God, refereed by Jesus and comforted by the Holy Spirit.

# Daily Reflections

**Pensive Moment:**

The next time you are in a difficult situation, remember that victory awaits on the other side of *through*.

**Prayer for Today:**

*Precious Father,*
*Thank you for the joy of parenting. Give me wisdom such that I may share with my child who turns to me in times of uncertainty.*

**Daily Thoughts/Goals:**

_____

_____

_____

_____

_____

_____

# The Church

Pastor preaching in the pulpit
Choir singing in the loft
Missionary praising in the corner
Deacon praying on the altar
Greeter welcoming at the door
Usher leading down the aisle
Attendant parking on the grounds
Elder sleeping in the rear

# The Black Church Experience

The charismatic preacher delivers the sermon
    Like God is conducting a performance evaluation

The spirit-filled choir bellows its sanctified souls
    With the force of a rocket at take-off

The rhythmic praise dancers move with grace and precision
    As if they're auditioning for "Dancing with the Stars"

The welcoming greeters embrace the guests
    Like Army cadets reuniting with family after basic training

The exuberant members sow tithes and offerings
    As if they're won the lottery.

# DAY 22

# It's Up to You

**Scripture Reading:**   Proverbs 4: 1-27

*Hear, my children, the instruction of a father, and give attention to know understanding; for I give you good doctrine: do not forsake my law. When I was my father's son, tender and the only one in the sight of my mother, he also taught me, and said to me: Let your heart retain my words; keep my commands, and live. Get wisdom! Get understanding! Do not forget, nor turn away from the words of my mouth.*   Proverbs 4: 1-5

**Daily Devotion:**

My daughter was excited for her appointment at the Division of Motor Vehicles to obtain her driver's license. It was a milestone in her life that she had waited for patiently. However, I was a little apprehensive that my youngest child would be a licensed driver. She studied, and to no surprise, passed both the written and road exams.

We stood in line at the agency behind a gentleman and his teenage son, waiting on my daughter's turn to pay the fee and check out with the license examiner. As the man and his son approached the desk, the examiner asked the young man if he wanted to pre-register to vote – a service offered by the driver license offices in our state. Not knowing how to answer the question, the son turned to his father and asked, "Should I?" Without hesitation, the father shrugged his shoulders and said, "It's up to you." The young man turned back to the examiner and responded, "No, I won't do that."

Suddenly, my jaw dropped, and my face contorted. This son asked his father whether he should register to vote, and the father had no advice to offer his son. He did not tell him how voting is a civic duty, and the way citizens elect leaders of our government. He did not share how voting is a privilege and, unlike this man, people of color and women were not always allowed to vote. He did not let his son know that voting rights are continuously being challenged and in jeopardy. No, he did not say any of that. He simply said to the son, "It's up to you."

I found this exchange between father and son quite disturbing. But even more unsettling was the fact that this young man wanted his father's advice, and this parent had none to give.

Children need and seek wise counsel from their parents. But all too often, parents have little to offer. Many young people are left to figure things out on their own - looking for answers in the wrong places and from people who do not have their best interests in mind. They turn to the internet, social media and even gangs trying to find what they are seeking.

Parental responsibilities go well beyond food, shelter and clothing. Children need love, prayer, instruction and discipline. They seek advice from parents when they don't know what to do. It is our responsibility to give them the guidance they need.

In our text, Solomon is calling on his sons to listen, but this passage speaks to all of us. Solomon was admonished by his father to take his words seriously – to keep his commands and live. Solomon emphasizes that parents are the dominant moral influencers and the instructors of their children. Nobody can replace the role of a parent to a child. But very often, people who have children are not ready to be parents. They want a child as a friend, a buddy, a company keeper - someone to give them the love they never had. But when God places the life of a child into their parents' care, He has given them a precious gift that not everyone has the pleasure of receiving.

A child is influenced by their parents. To help our children to become good decision-makers, Christian parents must be prepared to provide instruction and biblical answers to their questions. We must arm ourselves with resources to help our children navigate life as we pray with them and for them. Solomon encouraged his sons to seek wisdom. The Bible states, "If any of you lacks wisdom, he should ask God."

When it came time for the examiner to complete my daughter's paperwork to receive her license, she was asked the same question as the young man who preceded her. "Would you like to pre-register to vote?" She turned to me and said, "Should I?" Without hesitation, I responded, "Yes," and explained why. I did not tell her, "It's up to you."

# Daily Reflections

**Pensive Moment:**

Are you learning and providing wise counsel when your advice is needed?

**Prayer for Today:**

*Precious Father,*
*Thank you for the joy of parenting. Give me wisdom such that I may share with my child who turns to me in times of uncertainty.*

**Daily Thoughts/Goals:**

_____

_____

_____

_____

_____

_____

# Ode to the Harmonic Refined Lady

if admiration she wants    admiration she gets ---
she enters the room    everyone stops to stare
she is not fazed    by the attention.

with grace and elegance    she walks
and softly with confidence    she talks
the flair of her hair    the purple dress she wears
the twist of her hips    the paint on her lips
add    to her natural beauty.
she is grounded    in His Word
generous    with His resources
relentless    in her prayers
calm    in her spirit

she forgives    she is wise

conceited she's not    she knows what she's got
known by many    as a woman of plenty

she is    the daughter of the King.

# DAY 23

# You're Missing the Good Part

**Scripture Reading:**   Luke 10:38-42

*But Martha was distracted with much serving, and she approached Him and said, 'Lord, do You not care that my sister has left me alone? Therefore, tell her to help me.' And Jesus answered and said to her, 'Martha, Martha, you are worried and troubled about many things. But one thing is needed, and Mary has chosen that good part, which will not be taken away from her.* Luke 10:40-42

**Daily Devotion:**

In our text, Jesus entered the Town of Bethany and stopped at the home of Mary, Martha and Lazarus. He was close friends with these siblings. On this particular day, Martha invited Jesus over for dinner. Martha was known for her hospitality, and she was terribly busy in the kitchen preparing the meal. The scripture does not reveal what she was preparing, but fast forward to present day, and Martha would be cooking beef short ribs, oven-fried chicken, collard greens and cabbage, sour cream and chive potatoes, macaroni and cheese, buttered rolls, pound cake, peach cobbler and southern sweet tea because the Man of God was in the house.

Martha had much to do, and she wanted every part of the meal to be simply scrumptious. And while she enjoyed the meal preparation, Martha was very frustrated. She was in the kitchen cooking, and Mary was sitting at the feet of Jesus. According to the scriptures, Mary sat at the feet of Jesus quite often. In John 11:32, she fell to his feet when Lazarus died; in John 12:3, she anointed his feet with an alabaster box of expensive perfume; and in Luke, she is sitting at Jesus' feet yet again. To sit at the feet of Jesus was the position taken when you wanted to learn from the Master. And Mary was like a sponge. She wanted to saturate herself with everything Jesus had to say. But her failure to help her sister was upsetting to Martha. Mary was listening to the Word from the Lord while Martha was doing all the work preparing the meal.

In fact, Martha became so troubled that she said to Jesus, *"Lord, do you not care that my sister has left me to serve alone? Therefore, tell her to help me."* Martha's frustration so consumed her that she became agitated with Jesus and began telling Him what He should do. Yet, Jesus did not fret nor was He troubled by Martha's remarks. Instead, He calmly responded, *"Martha, Martha, you are worried about many things. But one thing is needed, and Mary has chosen the good part, which will not be taken away from her."*

Jesus was very appreciative of Martha's effort to provide food for his physical body. He was grateful for her hospitality, but Martha was distracted. Her distractions were causing her to miss her blessing. She was so focused on food preparation that she could not enjoy her guest, or the gift of God's Word that Jesus came to offer. He wanted Martha to understand that the instruction Mary was receiving was more important than the food Martha was preparing. Mary was receiving food for her soul, which would last her eternally.

In places of worship all across the world, there are Christians who are very much like Martha. They are so preoccupied with serving that they forget who they are serving and what they should learn in the process. In their busyness, they're missing the good part. If you serve the Kingdom of God in any capacity, you must be careful not to miss the good part. The work with the culinary ministry should not keep you so busy that you cannot hear and heed the sermon that the pastor delivers. You're missing the good part. The role of the finance committee, counting the money after service, should not interfere with your ability to seek prayer during the altar call at the conclusion of morning worship. You're missing the good part. The desire to welcome guests and make them feel comfortable, as part of the hospitality ministry, should not be so engaging that you cannot receive what you need from the worship experience. You're missing the good part.

Brides-to-be can become so enamored by the planning of the wedding that they stop short of investing in the marriage. They're missing the good part. Parents spend such an enormous amount of time providing instruction, guidance and discipline to their children that they forget to enjoy the blessings of youth and the laughter that a child brings. They're missing the good part. People go to funeral homes and establish pre-need arrangements, pick out caskets, dresses, suits, wigs, toupees and dentures. Yet, they take no thought of where they will spend eternity. They're missing the good part.

# Daily Reflections

**Pensive Moment:**

What are you prioritizing over time spent in the presence of God?

**Prayer for Today:**

*Precious Father,*
*Thank you for giving me a discerning spirit and the gift of prioritization, so I will not miss the good part.*

**Daily Thoughts/Goals:**

## Expectations

We were never allowed
to swear in momma's house    her house.

And when the storms came
we sat still, quiet
in the dark    respecting God's power.

Always saying blessing
before our meals and nobody took a bite of food   not before daddy.

And the sweet potato pies
were for company
we couldn't eat them    so we licked them.

# DAY 24

# Adversity is the Bridge to Growth

**Scripture Reading:**  Scriptures concerning adversity- **"the problem and the promise."**

*Many are the afflictions of the righteous, **but the Lord delivers him out of them all.*** Psalm 34:19

*We are **afflicted in every way**, **but not crushed;** perplexed, **but not driven to despair;** persecuted, **but not forsaken;** struck down **but not destroyed**.* 2 Corinthians 4:8-9

*But he said to me, **My grace is sufficient for you, for my power is made perfect in weakness**. Therefore, I will boast all the more gladly of **my weaknesses**, so that the **power of Christ may rest upon me**.* 2 Corinthians 12:9

*Beloved, **do not be surprised at the fiery trial when it comes upon you to test you**, as though something strange were happening to you. But rejoice insofar as you **share Christ's sufferings**, that you may also **rejoice and be glad when his glory is revealed**.* 1 Peter 4:12-13

*And after you **have suffered a little while**, the God of all grace, **who has called you to his eternal glory in Christ, will himself restore, confirm, strengthen and establish you**.* 1 Peter 5:10

*I know how **to be brought low**, and I know how to abound. In any and every circumstance, I have learned the secret of **facing** plenty and **hunger**, abundance and **need**. **I can do all things through Christ who strengthens me.*** Philippians 4:12-13

*Count it all joy, my brothers,* **when you meet trials of various kinds, for you know that the testing of your faith produces steadfastness.** James 1:2-3

*Blessed is the man who remains steadfast* **under trial,** *for when he has stood* **the test** *he will* **receive the crown of life, which God has promised to those who love him.** James 1:12

Adversity has a purpose in the lives of God's people. It is the vehicle of transportation that moves us toward maturity in our relationship with Christ.

Adversity leads to **GROWTH** because it:

**G**ets your attention.

**R**eveals your strengths and your weaknesses.

**O**pens your eyes to the challenges others face.

**W**ins faith over fear and shows you how to trust.

**T**akes away pride and self-sufficiency.

**H**elps prepare you for future service.

## Overcomers of Adversity – "a glimpse into their lives"

Adversity chooses a target. The target has a test.
The test leads to a testimony.

| The Target | The Test | The Testimony |
|---|---|---|
| Joseph – Jacob's son | Struggled at home; hated by his brothers who plotted to kill him; sold into slavery; accused by Potiphar's wife of sexual assault. | Persevered under adversity. Blessed those who cursed him and used him. Given a position in the King's court – second only to the King. Saved his family from famine. |
| Moses – Stuttering Shepherd | Slow of speech; doubted his abilities; faced Pharoah and ten plagues; dealt with stubborn people. | Brought redemption to God's people. Led the Israelites from Egypt to The Promised Land. Principle author of the Pentateuch- the foundational books of the Bible (Genesis, Exodus, Leviticus, Numbers, Deuteronomy) |
| Ruth – Loyal Servant | Honeymoon cut short; widowed woman; outsider in her in-laws' community; caregiver to her mother-in-law. | Met the God of Israel who changed her life. Faithfulness to her mother-in-law positioned her to marry a rich landowner named Boaz and receive the blessing of being listed in the lineage of Jesus. |
| David – Shepherd Boy | Anointed to be king at an early age; spent most of his life trying not to die at the hands of Saul; committed adultery and lost his first child. | Slew Goliath; honored as Israel's greatest King; provided a descendant whose name was Jesus, the Messiah, the Savior of the World. |
| Job – Good Man Under Consideration | Afflicted through no fault of his own; lost his wealth, his health and his children. Wife told him to "curse God and die." | God does not answer to anyone. Faithfulness has its rewards. Persevered through his difficulties. His life and possessions were restored. Received more than he lost. |
| Bleeding Woman – Person without a Name | Had a bleeding issue for 12 years. | Because of her faith and her persistence to get to Jesus, she received her healing. |
| Paul – Great Missionary | Great persecutor of Christians. Blinded by the Spirit of God on the road to Damascus. Had a thorn in his flesh that God would not remove. Whipped, beaten, shipwrecked and jailed. | Received conversion on the road to Damascus and became a passionate follower of Jesus Christ with a mission to spread the gospel though he suffered. Lived with the thorn in his flesh because God's grace was sufficient. Wrote 13 epistles of the New Testament. |

# Daily Reflections

**Pensive Moment:**

Pause to recall a time when you were the target, you endured a test, and you had a testimony.

**Prayer for Today:**

*Precious Father,*
*I thank you for allowing me to grow through my adversity such that my life will be a testimony of your goodness and your grace.*

**Daily Thoughts/Goals:**

_____

_____

_____

_____

_____

_____

# Her Child

I am my mother's child when
   I tell you
you don't look as big in that blue dress.

I am my mother's child when
   I work to find what's wrong
amidst everything that's right.

I am my mother's child when
   I bake a succulent pound cake
and tell you how to eat it.

I am my mother's child when
   I love you and sacrifice time for you
and pray that you notice.

I am my mother's child when I get on my knees to pray
   with all my failings
and realize that God forgives.

# DAY 25

# Let the Spirit Lead

**Scripture Reading:** Galatians 5: 16-26

*I say then: Walk in the Spirit, and you shall not fulfill the lust of the flesh.*
Galatians 5:16

**Daily Devotion:**

Upon retiring from public sector employment in 2013, I worked for a financial institution in the marketing department. Travel was required in this position during my first year, as I visited cities all across North Carolina promoting the institution's products.

On numerous occasions, I went to municipalities and counties where I had never been before. In these instances, I relied on my global positioning system, also known as GPS. From my mobile device, I used the virtual assistant to navigate me from place to place. However, there were times when I decided to go my own way, with hopes of discovering a shorter route. The GPS would reroute me. It knew when I made a wrong turn even when I did not. Based upon the address information entered, the device was designed to know when I needed help getting back on track. I could not fully explain or comprehend how the GPS worked at the time, but I didn't have to know. I was simply glad it was doing its job.

The GPS is to the vehicle what the Holy Spirit is to the believer. It guides. The Holy Spirit leads and guides the believer into the paths of righteousness, providing wisdom to make decisions in accordance with the Will of God.

The scripture states in Galatians 5:16, *"I say then: Walk in the Spirit, and you shall not fulfill the lust of the flesh."* For the Spirit and the flesh are in opposition – one to the other. Like a GPS, the Holy Spirit will speak, but you must be willing to heed that small directive voice. It will also reroute you if you make a wrong turn and need help getting back on track. But again, you must be willing to heed the voice. For scripture tells us, *"My sheep hear my voice and I know them, and they follow me."* Christ's sheep know how to hear, know what to ignore and know whom to follow because they spend time reading God's Word and establishing a relationship with Him.

If you are unable to recognize the presence and the voice of the Holy Spirit in your life, spend more time in prayer with God and consistently read His Word. He will strengthen the signal of your satellite and provide clearer reception.

We cannot always explain how the Holy Spirit works in every situation, but we don't have to understand it all. Just be grateful that God's presence is with you in the form of His Spirit and testify that it works.

# Daily Reflections

**Pensive Moment:**

What is causing interference, in your spiritual life, such that you cannot hear God speak?

**Prayer for Today:**

*Precious Father,*
*Allow me to be quick to listen so that I may receive your instruction with clarity of direction and purpose.*

**Daily Thoughts/Goals:**

_____

_____

_____

_____

_____

# DAY 26

# A Change Has Come Over Me

**Scripture Reading:**   Ezekiel 36:16-38

*I will give you a new heart and put a new spirit within you; I will take the heart of stone out of your flesh and give you a heart of flesh. I will put My Spirit within you and cause you to walk in My statutes, and you will keep My judgments and do them.*   Ezekiel 36:26-27

**Daily Devotion:**

The natural condition of the hearts of humans is deceitful. We are born into the world with a heart condition. It is one filled with sin and an innate desire to do what is not pleasing to God. Ever since the fall of Adam and Eve in the Garden of Eden, humans have had a proclivity to sin. But God desires to renew us spiritually and to change our hearts from a sinful nature to a heart that yearns after Him. This process is called circumcision and involves a spiritual removal of those sinful ways that hinder our loving, knowing and following the Will of God.

With some people, circumcision of the heart is immediate upon salvation. Yet, with others, it is a longer process. However, for all of us, conforming our hearts to the Will of God and His desire for our lives is a lifelong journey as we progress from salvation through the process of sanctification.

In my daily walk with Christ, I see proof consistently that I am not the same person that I used to be. As I briefly glance in the rearview mirror of life, I see a trail of evidence that I have left some old things behind. Each day, my thoughts, my words and my deeds are more aligned with God's Will for my life. With a feeling of gratitude, I die to sin daily.

Recently, while shopping at the grocery store, I had an experience that reminded me of the presence of the Holy Spirit in my life. It was Sunday morning. I was headed home after worship service at church. I stopped at the store to purchase a few groceries needed for the day. Having less than ten items, I used self-check-out, which is rare for me. Carefully, I scanned all my items, or so I thought. When I rolled the cart to my car to put the groceries inside, I noticed that the sweet rolls were not in a plastic grocery bag. Instead, they were laying at the bottom of the cart. I looked at my receipt, and the purchase did not appear. I had not scanned the bar code on the rolls. And somehow, I was able to exit the store without any alert. I paused. The store was busy. The parking lot was crowded. I was ready to go home. Nobody knew that I didn't scan the bar code. It was just a package of rolls. Nobody cared. It was a mistake. But I knew I did not pay. And yes, it was just a package of rolls. But I cared.

I felt that gentle tug of the Holy Spirit. I stood in the parking lot, and for just a moment, I could not move. I knew what I needed to do. So, I put the other items in the car, replaced the cart and took the sweet rolls back inside the store. I approached the clerk at the self-out, told her what happened and paid for the rolls.

I was born with a heart condition, but a change has come over me.

# Daily Reflections

**Pensive Moment:**

When doing the right thing is not your first thought, are you willing to push past your flesh to please God?

**Prayer for Today:**

*Precious Father,*
*I am grateful for my new heart and the Holy Spirit that helps me to hear and to obey even when it is not convenient.*

**Daily Thoughts/Goals:**

_____

_____

_____

_____

_____

_____

# DAY 27

# Lessons Learned from a Widow

**Scripture Reading:**   1 Kings 17: 8-16

*So, she said, 'As the Lord your God lives, I do not have bread, only a handful of flour in a bin and a little oil in a jar; and see, I am gathering a couple of sticks that I may go in and prepare it for myself and my son, that we may eat it and die.'* 1 Kings 17:12

**Daily Devotion:**

In the 17th Chapter of the Book of First Kings, we meet a prophet named Elijah, a spokesman for God, who prophesied a drought upon the nation of Israel. There is no rain in sight, and famine is all over the land. Elijah's food supply is being sustained by God, but his present source is running out. Based upon God's instruction, Elijah visits a place called Zarephath to get food from a nameless widow and her son. But when he arrives, like others, the widow has nothing to eat. Just a handful of flour and a little oil. She tells the prophet that she is preparing to make a cake for her and her son. Realizing that starvation is only one meal away, they are preparing to lie down and die.

Elijah beckons her, and lets her know, per God's instructions, she is to feed him first. The widow is hesitant but heeds the voice of the Lord through the prophet and feeds Elijah. Her faith was tested, but her act of obedience provides flour in her barrel that does not run out, and the oil never fails. She eats her meal and never misses another.

There are several lessons that we can glean from the story of this widow:

- ❖ God uses unlikely people frequently to accomplish His purpose. This vessel was a woman and a widow. In her culture at that time, she wasn't worthy of anybody's attention, so there was no expectation that she would be used by God.
- ❖ God shows His mercy to Jews and Gentiles. This woman was from Zarephath. She was a Gentile. Yet, her faith was enough to receive a reward.
- ❖ God requires obedience. The Widow at Zarephath received her miracle because she obeyed in faith and fed Elijah first. She didn't make excuses. She hesitated but proceeded and followed the instructions of the prophet.
- ❖ God teaches that when you're in need, meet a need and your needs will be met. This woman had a need, and though she was concerned for her livelihood and that of her son, she attended to Elijah first. When we are able to focus on the needs of others, despite our own, God's help is on the way.

It matters not the bleakness of your situation. God brings light to darkness. Like the widow, you may be ready to eat your last meal and die. But don't make the cake too soon. Your breakthrough, your turning point, may be just a prophet away. God can send a messenger straight to you, but you must be prepared to hear the voice and receive God's Word.

The Widow at Zarephath heard the voice of the Lord through the Prophet Elijah, and she followed his instructions. The next time you find yourself in a predicament with no good end in sight, remember the nameless widow. She could be you.

# Daily Reflections

**Pensive Moment:**

How many blessings have you missed because God spoke to someone, that you could not hear, with a Word that you did not want to receive?

**Prayer for Today:**

*Precious Father,*
*Thank you for meeting my needs as I share my provision with others.*

**Daily Thoughts/Goals:**

_____

_____

_____

_____

_____

_____

# DAY 28

# Looking Good on the Way to Hell

**Scripture Reading:**   1 Samuel 16:1-13

*But the Lord said to Samuel, 'Do not look at his appearance or at his physical stature because I have refused him. For the Lord does not see as man sees; for man looks at the outward appearance, but the Lord looks at the heart.'*   1 Samuel 16:7

**Daily Devotion:**

Having rejected Saul as king, God sent the prophet Samuel on a mission to Bethlehem to anoint Israel's next king from the house of Jesse. Knowing the stature of Saul, Samuel imagined in his mind the look of the next king – impressive in appearance, tall with broad shoulders and very handsome.

However, God gave Samuel instructions to not look at the outward appearance of the person He selected. God wanted Samuel to understand that He did not choose His servants according to their outward appearances. Instead, He considered their hearts.

When Samuel arrived at Jesse's house, he met seven of Jesse's eight sons. He looked over the seven, and none of them was God's chosen one to be Israel's next king. Samuel asked Jesse if all his sons were present. That's when Jesse called David, his youngest son, who was working in the pasture tending sheep. When Samuel saw David, God told him immediately that David was the chosen one – Israel's next king.

According to the Bible, David was good-looking but a tender of sheep who was reddish in color with bright eyes. Not the likely candidate by position nor stature. David wasn't Samuel's choice, but according to his heart, he belonged to God.

Unlike God, human beings are obsessed with outward appearances – physical characteristics – the least of which concerns our Heavenly Father. Nothing about the way we look impresses God. He focuses on the condition of our hearts, our faith in Him and our spiritual growth – wanting only for us to make the conscious choice to accept Him as the Savior of the World so we may live with Him eternally.

Knowing that God places such little value on physical attractiveness, it becomes incredible to think about how much money we spend on outward appearances. Dieting, joining fitness centers, having weight loss surgeries, purchasing cosmetic and beauty products – all to improve our physical attractiveness which is not on God's list of priorities. Many people, so consumed with themselves, believe that taking such measures correlates to pleasing God and living a healthy life.

Billions of dollars each year are spent on dieting and diet products with millions of Americans going on fad diets. Celebrities tout various weight loss products and get paid enormous amounts of money for being able to convince those who desire to lose weight for reasons that have nothing to do with being physically or spiritually healthy that these products work. But nearly two-thirds of Americans continue to be overweight or obese because quick fixes don't last and risks to health are often involved. And diet products are not the only big-ticket purchases that are made in an effort to acquire or maintain a youthful appearance. Cosmetics, beauty products and unnecessary medical procedures absorb much of the American budget, with the United States leading other nations spending billions in this industry as well.

God desires for His people to take care of their bodies, both inside and out. And it is perfectly natural to want to look your best. But being preoccupied with physical attractiveness with little to no regard for spiritual health and well-being is a road paved to hell with many travelers.

Life on earth is temporary. Beauty fades. Bodies decay. No fixes – short or long-term – will change that immutable fact. The body parts that were once perky will droop, and the parts that stood at attention will pay attention no more. But a soul that is saved lives forever.

Confess your sins. Accept Jesus as Savior. Develop a personal relationship with Him. Love each other. Assemble yourselves with like-minded believers in praise, worship and service. Give charitably.

And when this life concludes and Jesus returns, your spirit will connect with your glorified body, and you will live life eternal.

# Daily Reflections

**Pensive Moment:**

Have you ever allowed vanity to take precedence over your spiritual well-being?

**Prayer for Today:**

*Precious Father,*
*Thank you for showing me how to keep my temple healthy from the inside out.*

**Daily Thoughts/Goals:**

_____

_____

_____

_____

_____

_____

# Journey to Healing

It's Thanksgiving Day. The children and I are getting ready to join our families for dinner – both yours and mine. A family tradition.

Over nine years since God took you home.
Still grappling with that. You were only 48, one month shy of your birthday.

Pregnant with our daughter when your illness was revealed.
For the nine years you had with her, a sick dad was most of all she knew.
But a great dad you were.

I remember the incredulous look on the doctors' faces when your diagnosis was confirmed.
Thirty-nine-year-old male with congestive heart failure.

Our son, only seven – too young to understand how life was about to change.
What a great caregiver he was to you. Never complaining about having to bring you whatever you needed – water, medicine, your Bible or the plastic containers when the excess fluid in your body needed some place to go.

Lifestyle changes, pills, pacemaker, left ventricular assist device, heart transplant.
You tried it all, but your dying was not for lack of your will.
God's will must be accomplished.

Though I would like to ask God some questions.

Why did this happen? Could He have not given you more time? We served and trusted Him. Is this the reward for obedience? How am I supposed to take care of two children without their father? Who will teach our son how to drive and walk our daughter down the aisle on the day of her wedding? How will I ever explain your death to them?

In my moment of weakness, I questioned God.

But my weakness did not last. I reflected on the things that kept us together for 19 years – our love for each other, our love for God and our belief in His Sovereignty.

Though neither of us expected death would come so soon, we stayed until death did us do part. We prepared our hearts and minds for this day. And because of that, I have faith in what the Bible states in 2 Corinthians 5:8, *"We are confident, yes, well pleased rather to be absent from the body and to be present with the Lord."*

With that, I continue to get ready for dinner, making one of your favorites – sweet potato casserole. It will be a great day of Thanksgiving. You are forever with us.

# DAY 29

# The Need for GAP Protection

**Scripture Reading:** Ezekiel 22:23-31

*So, I sought for a man among them who would make a wall and stand in the gap before Me on behalf of the land, that I should not destroy it; but I found no one.* Ezekiel 22:30

**Daily Devotion:**

In June 2016, three months before his 84th birthday, my dad decided to buy a new Ford F-150 Truck – his favorite vehicle. My mom, my sister and I were not at all pleased with this purchase for several reasons. But my dad didn't consult us, and he didn't need our permission.

My sister and I prayed for God's protection over him and his new vehicle. Two months after the purchase and before the second payment was due, my dad was involved in an accident at an intersection. It was early evening and dusk dark. He did not see the car coming and proceeded to cross the highway causing a crash where he was deemed at fault. By the grace of God, the driver of the other vehicle was not hurt, and my dad walked away with only bruises from the airbag. But the truck was a total loss. Thankfully, he had GAP insurance coverage.

GAP is an acronym that stands for "guaranteed asset protection." It pays the difference between the amount you owe on a vehicle and the actual cash value that the insurance company pays if the vehicle is in a covered accident and declared a total loss. Because of this insurance, my dad walked away from the total loss of a new truck owing nothing.

My family was so thankful that he was not seriously injured and equally grateful that he had GAP insurance. This resulted in no further out-of-pocket expenses. For my sister and I, GAP took on another meaning – "God Answers Prayer."

In today's devotion, the reference to gap means a hole or opening in a space. As I read the text, I can almost see imaginatively a wall with a hole in it. In biblical times, a wall or fortress was the best means of protection from the enemy. If the wall was breached, it left a gap which gave the enemy room to enter. Defenders of the wall would have to band together to keep the enemy out – providing protection – until the gap was repaired. Failure to repair the opening meant destruction for the city.

In Ezekiel chapter 22, the sins of Israel are brought before us. The leaders were wicked, and God planned to scatter the nation as a result of their disobedience. But He was willing to spare them destruction if HE could find one person to stand in the gap, that is, provide the protection needed. He had no volunteers who were willing to intercede and to be a defender. Destruction was imminent. And in this case, judgment had to fall.

However, the Bible is full of warriors in these ancient times who risked it all to stand in the gap for others – people who interceded and pleaded for God's mercy.

- ❖ Moses, the Hebrew prophet chosen to bring redemption to the children of Israel, stood in the gap for them when they became impatient and built a golden calf to worship. He pleaded with God on their behalf.
- ❖ Abraham, the father of all nations, interceded for the sinful City of Sodom.
- ❖ Paul, the Apostle of Grace, prayed for Israel's salvation.

But the Master of all those who stood in the gap was Jesus who gave His life and paid the penalty for the remission of our sins – all the while forgiving those responsible for His suffering. While hanging from an old rugged cross and bleeding from his side, Jesus uttered, *"Father, forgive them, for they know not what they do."* Because of Jesus, we have victory over death and owe nothing. He continues to intercede on our behalf.

## Daily Reflections

**Pensive Moment:**

Have you ever considered that every prayer you offer for someone in need provides protection?

**Prayer for Today:**

*Precious Father,*
*Thank you for my protection. I know that you answer prayer.*

**Daily Thoughts/Goals:**

_____

_____

_____

_____

_____

# DAY 30

# He Paid Full Price

**Scripture Reading:**  1 Corinthians 6:12-20

*For you were bought at a price; therefore, glorify God in your body and in your spirit, which are God's.*  1 Corinthians 6:20

**Daily Devotion:**

Anyone who knows me is aware that I like shopping for sales. Bargain shopping and securing deals is not for everyone, but I don't like paying full price for anything. Whether it is clothes, household goods, services or entertainment, I am always looking for the best quality at the lowest price.

Initially, I check to see if the item is on sale. And if I'm shopping in-store, I ask about coupons and look for them online. If not, I examine the item thoroughly to make sure there are not any defects. Small defects can often lead to an item being discounted. In addition, some retailers will allow their employees to share their discounts with customers if there is a "friends and family day," so I inquire about that as well – taking advantage of all opportunities that are available to save money.

If I decide to purchase the item, cash or credit, I make sure that I understand how the return policy works just in case I change my mind about the purchase, large or small. In retail shopping transactions, prudent shoppers consider these things because they want the best value for the money they pay.

However, over 2000 years ago, a purchase was made on your behalf and mine, but the transaction went down a little differently. The buyer did not ask if the item was on sale. He did not ask the sales associate to check the coupon of the day or try to find a coupon online. He did not examine the item for defects or seek the "friends and family" discount. He did not request information about the return policy. He did not use cash or purchase with credit. This transaction was not made "COD," which means "collect on delivery." Instead, the transaction was "LOD," which means "life on delivery." The buyer was Jesus. He gave His life for us to be delivered from the penalty of sin.

Jesus knew that He was purchasing damaged goods, but they were beautifully and wonderfully made by the Creator who makes no mistakes. He was aware that it doth yet appear what the product shall be in the hands of its Architect. So, Jesus sealed the transaction by paying with his life. No receipt necessary.

As a buyer, Jesus was immeasurably different than others who have made purchases. Buyers are usually received with delight. But Jesus was despised and rejected by men. He was a suffering Savior who was familiar with grief, wounded for the crimes we committed and bruised for our immoral behavior. He bore pain for us to enjoy forgiveness and peace. He was beaten so we could die to our sins and live for righteousness. This buyer Jesus was oppressed and afflicted and brought like a lamb waiting to be killed. Yet, He was willing to pay His life as ransom for you and for me. At a site called Golgotha – the place of the transaction – Jesus hung on a rugged cross and paid the penalty of sin with His life, purchasing us, so we may live eternally.

Jesus charges us nothing, but we owe Him everything. Our lives are not our own. We belong to Him because He paid full price.

# Daily Reflections

**Pensive Moment:**

How will you show your gratitude for the price Jesus paid for you?

**Prayer for Today:**

*Precious Father,*
*Thank you for giving your life for me and not waiting for me to be discounted or to go on sale.*

**Daily Thoughts/Goals:**

_____

_____

_____

_____

_____

_____

# DAY 31

# The Goal is to Go Home

**Scripture Reading:**   Hebrews 11:13-26

*But now they desire a better, that is, a heavenly country. Therefore, God is not ashamed to be called their God, for He has prepared a city for them.*
                                                               Hebrews 11:16

**Daily Devotion:**

When it was time for my daughter to learn to drive, we were blessed to have one of our friends, a retired chief of police, to help her become comfortable with the mechanics of the vehicle and to provide her with basic instruction before taking the official driver's education course. This man had been one of her father's closest friends and a groomsman in our wedding. I knew she would be comfortable with him, especially in the absence of her dad.

During one of her driving lessons, she met and talked to a police officer in our city. My daughter posed situational questions to the officer. He was not only knowledgeable, but he was patient with her and explained driving laws and safe driving practices. Specifically, my daughter wanted to know how to respond to a police officer if she was stopped but did not believe she had committed a violation. The officer told her that a lot of authority came with the badge that a police officer carried. And while most officers were in the business to help people, not every patrol officer had the best intentions – what we all know to be an indisputable fact. He told my daughter to keep in mind that "the goal is to go home." That she should respect the officer's authority and position and do what they asked her to do, which included keeping her hands visible or exiting the vehicle, if requested. The goal was to get home safely. He explained to her if the officer did anything that she believed violated her rights, she should make notes and address the matter through the appropriate channels at a later date. But in the moment, her "goal is to go home," and that meant following the officer's instructions.

I began thinking about what the officer said in the context of our Christian lives. We live on earth. We encounter situations with people on the roads of life. There are times we experience God-ordained traffic stops that pull us over. We feel handcuffed by poorly managed finances, failing health and broken relationships. But if we have faith in God, respect His authority and His position, follow His direction and keep our hands visible by lifting them up in praise, God will guide us and take us home.

Home, the place that God has prepared. Home, the other country awaiting us and the dwelling place of the Heavenly Father. Home, the city where our citizenship will not be called into question, where voting rights are not in jeopardy, where there is no fake news. Home, the place of no accidents, no illnesses and no diseases; no mask-wearing, no physical distancing, no vaccinations. Home, the place where love abounds. Home, the place of healing. Home, the place of no more suffering, no more sadness, no more tears, no more death. Home, where everything is new, and we can drink eternally from the flowing fountain of living water.

If you desire a better country, the goal is to go home.

# Daily Reflections

**Pensive Moment:**

Have you confessed your belief in God as your Personal Savior so that you may inherit eternal life?

**Prayer for Today:**

*Precious Father,*
*Thank you for giving me a spirit of obedience to accept You as Personal Savior, so I may go home.*

**Daily Thoughts/Goals:**

_____

_____

_____

_____

_____

# 31 DAYS of a Servant's HEART

## Desiree Smith White

# ABOUT THE
## *Author*

# About the Author
## *Desiree Smith White*

# About the Author
## *Desiree Smith White*

Desiree Smith White is a woman with a genuine love of the Lord and His people and a heart to serve. As a preacher of the gospel of Jesus Christ, she brings to the pulpit an understandable explanation of the gospel, a sense of humor and a commitment to *"keep it real."*

Desiree graduated from the University of North Carolina at Chapel Hill with a Bachelor of Science Degree in Industrial Relations. She dedicated 30 years of her career to public service. In addition to being a Tar Heel, Desiree is a member of the Wolfpack. She holds a certificate in professional writing from North Carolina State University.

Desiree's love of language, both written and spoken, became evident at an early age when one of her teachers referred to her as an "avid conversationalist." Desiree proceeded to use her talent for writing as a columnist for the local newspaper during her senior year in high school. But it didn't stop there. When Desiree was called into the gospel ministry, her natural ability to communicate with clarity offered her an opportunity to connect with people at different levels, build trust, develop meaningful relationships and change lives.

Though Desiree has always enjoyed putting pen to paper, it became healing for her when she found herself in the corner of a widow after the death of her husband. Her most difficult oral and written assignment came when she delivered his eulogy as her young children sat among the mourners of family and friends.

In 2018, Desiree founded *Heart to Serve Ministries* based upon the scripture Matthew 23:11, *"The greatest among you will be your servant."* Led by the Word of God, she seeks to provide motivation, encouragement and inspiration to widows and single moms and serve as a resource to those in need.

Desiree is an associate minister at The Ebenezer Church in Burlington, North Carolina, where she assumes several roles in leadership. Desiree enjoys preaching God's Word, motivational speaking, writing and spending time with family and friends. She resides in Mebane, North Carolina, and is the mother of a son and a daughter. *31 Days of a Servant's Heart* is her first published book.

# Heart to Serve
## MINISTRIES
"THE GREATEST AMONG YOU WILL BE YOUR SERVANT."
Matthew 23:11

Post Office Box 344
Mebane, NC 27302
heartserve88@gmail.com

SHEROPUBLISHING.COM

Made in the USA
Columbia, SC
08 June 2024